THE STORY OF SIR PETER BLAKE

About the author

Tessa Duder has published more than 40 books, including the award-winning *Alex* quartet, non-fiction, biographies, anthologies and plays. A champion swimmer as a teenager, she has enjoyed sailing in various dinghies, classic yachts and as a volunteer in the youth ship *Spirit of New Zealand*. Her awards include the Storylines Margaret Mahy Medal, the OBE and an Honorary Doctorate from the University of Waikato. She has four children, two grandchildren and has lived in Auckland most of her life. More information can be found on her website www.tessaduder.com.

THE STORY OF SIR PETER BLAKE

TESSA DUDER

LIBRO INTERNATIONAL

FOUNDATION PARTNER

 |  |

THE
SIR PETER BLAKE
TRUST
Leadership in Action

Published with the support of The Sir Peter Blake Trust

Published by Libro International, an imprint of Oratia Media Ltd, 783 West Coast Road, Oratia, Auckland 0604, New Zealand (www.librointernational.com).

Copyright © Tessa Duder 2012
The copyright holder asserts her moral rights in the work.

This book is copyright. Except for the purposes of fair reviewing, no part of this publication may be reproduced or transmitted in any form or by any means, whether electronic, digital or mechanical, including photocopying, recording, any digital or computerised format, or any information storage and retrieval system, including by any means via the Internet, without permission in writing from the publisher. Infringers of copyright render themselves liable to prosecution.

ISBN 978-1-877514-42-5

First published 2012

Front cover image: A very happy Peter Blake at the official Team New Zealand ceremony to unveil the keels of the New Zealand boats for the America's Cup, February 2000. Photo: Christian Février
Back cover image: A bicycle from Seamaster *proves handy for getting around to investigate the Antarctic wildlife. Photo: Don Robertson*
Back cover quote from Mark Orams, crew member on Steinlager 2, *and colleague for the America's Cup campaigns and blakeexpeditions.*

The author has made every effort to verify factual information in this work, and accepts responsibility in the case of any error.

Printed in China by Nordica

Contents

Acknowledgements		6
Map		8
1	The sea in his blood	10
2	Building boats, learning the ropes	18
3	'Sea Fever' and twice around the world	26
4	*Ceramco*: 'The Porcelain Rocket Ship'	34
5	*Lion New Zealand*: 'The Urban Assault Vehicle'	48
6	Around Australia on *Steinlager 1*	57
7	Whitbread glory on *Steinlager 2*	66
8	Around the World in 80 Days	80
9	'The America's Cup is now New Zealand's Cup!'	94
10	'The America's Cup is *still* New Zealand's Cup!'	105
11	Ambassador for the environment	114
12	Epilogue	126
Sir Peter Blake — honours and awards		130
Glossary		133

Acknowledgements

Numerous magazine articles, newspaper stories and more than a few books have been written about Sir Peter Blake, resulting in a mountain of material available to anyone re-telling the story of his life.

For this book I have drawn mostly upon several key publications, and I thank their authors most sincerely.

Primarily I thank Alan Sefton for his full-length biography, *Sir Peter Blake: An Amazing Life* (Penguin Books New Zealand, 2004). For anyone wishing to read a more detailed account of Peter Blake's life, his yachting achievements and his environmental work, this is the single best resource.

I have also quoted from several other sources, including Lady Pippa Blake's generous and moving memoirs entitled *Journey*, published by Penguin in 2012 to mark the tenth anniversary of Sir Peter's death; *Blake: Leader*, by Mark Orams who was a *Steinlager 2* crew member and long-time Blake associate (Random House New Zealand, 2009); *Sir Peter Blake: A Pictorial Salute*, by Richard Becht (Hodder Moa Beckett, 2001); and Peter Blake's own handsomely illustrated memoirs, *Adventurer*, published 1996 in France after he won the Trophée Jules Verne for the fastest non-stop circumnavigation of the world.

From these principal sources have come quotes from other key figures in the Blake story, principally Sir Robin Knox-Johnston, Les Williams, Sir Tom Clark, Sir Douglas Myers, Grant Dalton, Mark Orams and Mike Quilter.

I'm grateful to Peter's brother Tony Blake who kindly shared memories of their childhood. For their helpful comments on the manuscript I thank Lady Pippa Blake and her family; Deputy Chair of the Sir Peter Blake Trust Ross Blackman; and CEO Shelley Campbell and Programme Director Hannah Prior. Thanks are also due to Peter Dowling and Carolyn Lagahetau of Oratia Media for their support and patience.

For help in sourcing the pictures used in the book, special thanks are due to Lady Pippa Blake, Peter's brother Tony Blake and sister Jan Stokes, the Sir Peter Blake Trust, Penguin Books, Peter Montgomery, Don Robertson, Martin Foster, Christian Février, Ben Watson (*North Shore Times*) and George Johns.

Tessa Duder
Auckland, March 2012

Note Throughout this book yachts are referred to as 'she'. This was the traditional usage in Sir Peter's time, and it seems wrong to call his many extraordinary and beloved creations, from *Bandit* through *Black Magic* to his last boat *Seamaster*, by the neutral 'it' now more common. So 'she' they are!

Map of key places

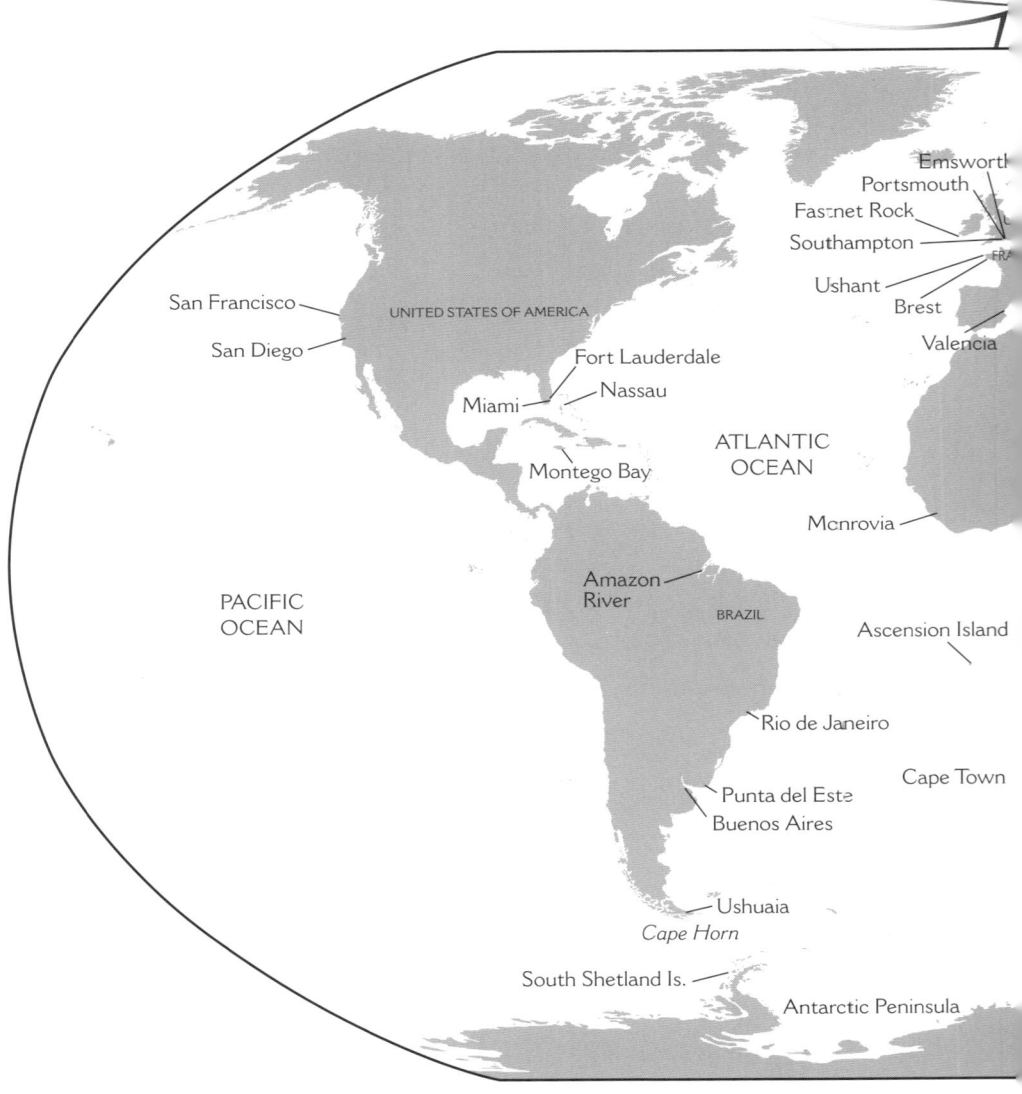

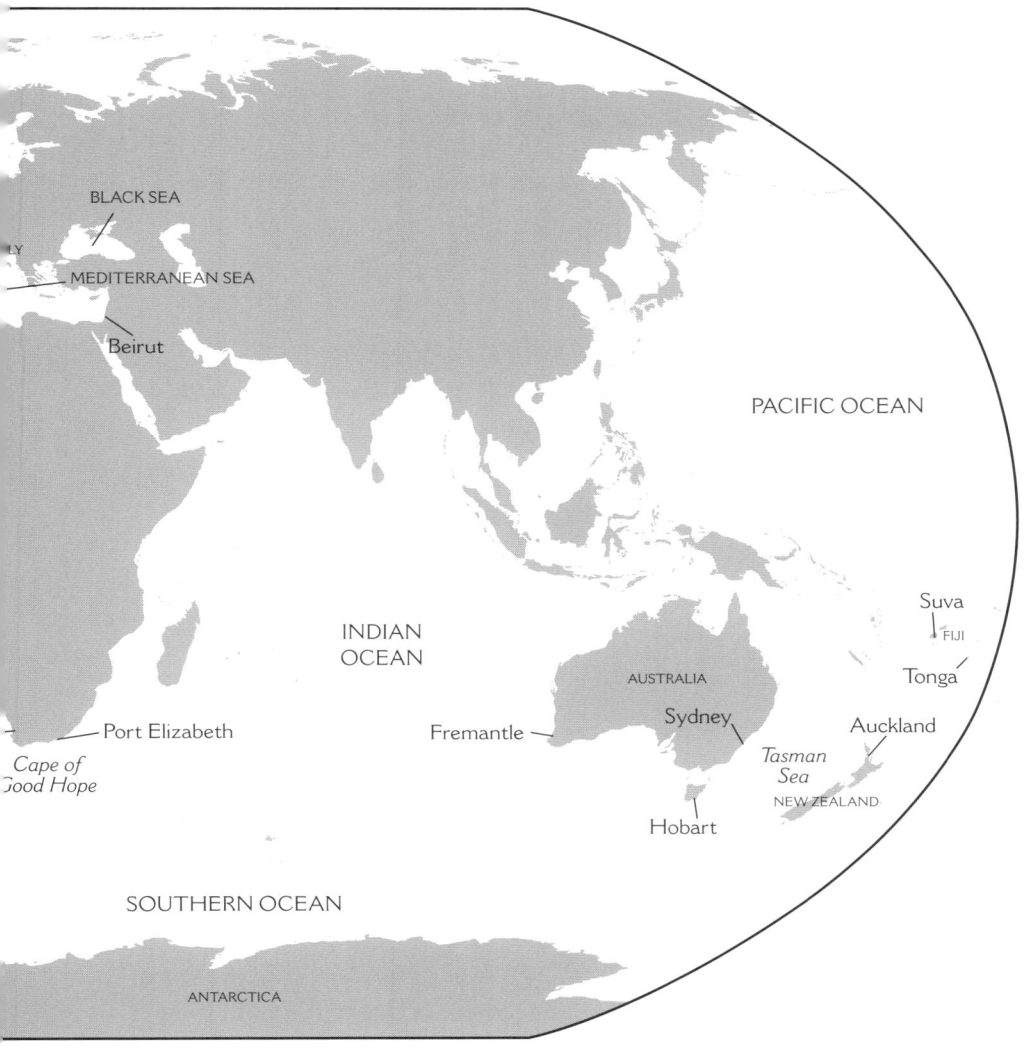

1

The sea in his blood

Peter Blake was surely born with the sea in his blood.

The Blakes were a typical Auckland sailing family. Both Peter's father Brian and his uncle Don owned keelers and were keenly competitive 'yachties' on the Waitemata Harbour and around the Hauraki Gulf.

In wartime, a few years before Peter was born, Brian commanded naval gunboats off the English coasts and an air-sea rescue craft in the Pacific. Peter's mother, Joyce, the great-granddaughter of a sea captain, had grown up in Point Chevalier crewing for her brothers on the Waitemata. She was a capable crew at a time when the sport of yachting was usually an all-male affair. Before he went off to war, Brian and Joyce often enjoyed sailing together.

Peter was born in 1948, their second child. Blond and blue-eyed as they come, he didn't have to go far to get afloat. The back lawn of the family home in Bayswater sloped down into the Waitemata.

As a child, Peter's first experiences on the water probably included learning to row the family's first boat, a modest clinker dinghy, about 10 feet (3 metres) long and made of wood, as was usual at that time.

After school, weekends and holidays, Peter and his younger brother, Tony, spent hours exploring the shallow waters of Shoal Bay or sailing the miniature square-riggers they constructed out of wooden banana boxes. Summer camping holidays on the family's section next door to their grandparents' place at Mairangi Bay were spent messing round in whatever boats they could find.

> *Driftwood and mussel shells, crabs scurrying across the mud, even a seahorse once: each new tide across the mud flats of Bayswater where I was raised, brought new treasures ... We found a small derelict dinghy once washed up on the shore, bought a dollar's worth of canvas from the sailmaker down the road and Mum made a squaresail for it on her sewing machine. Dragging the boat along the beach against the wind, we then jumped in, sailing downwind.* (Peter Blake, Adventurer, *p. 8*)

After the wooden dinghy, the next family boat had a pedigree and a name. Brian built a Frostply dinghy, 11 foot 6 inches long (3.4 metres) with an outboard motor, for his growing family. In it, they could take more ambitious rowing adventures and fishing trips. Mostly, though, the *Japeto* (for Janet-Peter-Tony) was for sailing. Peter would often be allowed to take the helm.

Japeto, *seen on the left, was used for all sorts of expeditions including fishing, exploring and, of course, sailing.*

Soon, races were being held with other families who lived near the water. Peter took to racing like a duck to water. Not for him the more usual boys' games like cricket and rugby. He wanted to be out on the water, testing his skills against other sailors and the elements.

Brian, perhaps beginning to recognise a rare passion in his son and seeing an instinct and talent for sailing, got out his hammer and saw and set to work again. Eight-year-old Peter became captain of his own ship, the *Pee Bee*. She was one of the famous P-class training yachts, all of seven-and-a-half feet (2.3 metres) long. In *Pee Bee*, Peter had his first taste of official racing at the nearby Takapuna Boating Club. However, *Pee Bee* wasn't just for racing round the buoys. Size was no barrier to this intrepid explorer. Many years later, Peter wrote:

> *Friends and I used to go all over Waitemata Harbour in our Ps together, and sometimes ended up being blown into the mangroves around the edge. We explored all the creeks near home. I can remember sailing on evenings after school, the sun going down on the water. I'd sail through flotillas of water birds. Really peaceful: I had as good a time then as sailing around the world years later.* (Adventurer, p. 10)

Dinghy racing at the Takapuna Boating Club was fiercely competitive.

> ## Why the P-class?
>
> Why is the snub-nosed P-class dinghy famous for being the first 'serious' boat of nearly all New Zealand's top sailors, including world-famous professionals such as Sir Peter Blake, Sir Russell Coutts, Chris Dickson, Leslie Egnot, Grant Dalton and Dean Barker?
>
> Perhaps because it's a 'pig of a thing' to sail! If you can sail a P-class well, it's said, you can sail anything. It's fast, tricky, and prone to capsizing.
>
> In New Zealand, every January hundreds of ambitious boys and girls from about age eight upwards gather to contest the regional Tanner Cup and then the national Tauranga Cup. Doing well in these events is the first step towards selection for an Olympic Games or becoming a world-travelling professional offshore sailor. The competition is fierce.
>
> The P-class design originated in 1920, when a civil engineer called Harry Highet built the wooden prototype near Whangarei. However, it wasn't until three years later when Highet was living near Tauranga harbour with his family, that the tiny P-class craft, with its single sail, started to become popular. The first Ps sported a gunter rig and were known as the 'Tauranga' class, but later they had a Bermudan sail and became known as the 'P' (primary) class.
>
> Today's P-class can be made of plywood or fibreglass and the masts are made of aluminium or carbon fibre. Strict rules mean that the dimensions and total weight of all boats are very similar to ensure fair racing.

However, *Pee Bee* was not to last because Peter was unusually tall for his age. In her, he recalled, my 'knees kept coming up beneath my chin whenever I ducked beneath the boom to come about.' His dad realised that before too long his lanky son would need a considerably bigger boat.

This was *Tango*, a plywood Z-class, 12 foot 6 inches (3.6 metres) long. However, she wasn't the usual white-painted, white-sailed 'Zeddie'. Peter, now 10 years old, wanted something with a bit more dash, even if, as brother Tony recalls, he did have to put lead bars inside to bring crew and yacht up to the required weight.

Zeddies and other small classes line up for the start.

Lead bars or not, there was no mistaking *Tango*'s black hull and brilliant orange sails, usually near the front of the Z-class racing fleet. Or the Blake brothers out there in a fresh southwesterly, tacking across the harbour to hoist the striped orange-and-black spinnaker in the lee of the city wharves, to fly back across the waves to Bayswater, going like a rocket. Sometimes they'd end up with a spectacular capsize, with the mast dug into the harbour mud and a mess of sails and rigging to sort out. Or they'd sail over to Rangitoto, the circular volcanic island that guards the entrance to the Waitemata Harbour, and hike up to the top.

The boys had two basic rules for all their adventuring: wear lifejackets and be home in time for dinner.

The racing bug, specially, was beginning to bite. At age 13, Peter came close to winning the Zeddies' national championship, the Cornwall Cup. Tony says, 'he was pipped at the post, but I think that's when the family began to realise his potential.' Going out for a sail was easy. There was the club close by where dinghies could be stored and the brothers could quickly prepare for an after-school or weekend spin.

Peter enjoyed an ideal childhood. The family was comfortably off, but not wealthy. His father, Brian, who worked as an art director for an advertising agency, was a highly competent seaman and boat-builder. Peter's mother, Joyce, understood both the joys and the risks of sailing. Their family life was close and cooperative; they frequently enjoyed card and board games together and everyone 'got stuck in' when an extension was built on to their Bayswater home.

> *I think our family ties were installed in us naturally. No one shouted, Mum and Dad helping us a lot. From quite an early age I knew that you could actually win, not so much by coming first, as by knowing you have done your best.* (Adventurer, p. 8)

When Peter was around 11 his parents sold the Mairangi Bay cliff-top section, giving them enough money to buy a keelboat for family weekends and holidays cruising round the Hauraki Gulf. *Ngarangi* was 30 feet (9.14 metres) long, just big enough to accommodate parents and four children.

> **"** *I had as good a time then as sailing around the world years later.* **"**

However, she proved a rather slow and unsatisfactory keeler to sail. Two summers after her purchase the Blakes scraped together every last cent of their savings to buy a handsome ketch they had often seen, and greatly admired, coming into anchorages around the Gulf.

The ketch was the handsome *Ladybird*, designed by famous Devonport designer Bert Woollacott. Ten years earlier she had won the first race between Hobart (Tasmania) and Auckland. *Ladybird* was the boat that, one day, Peter hoped to enjoy in his retirement.

> *She was just under 34 foot (10.2 metres) long, varnished timber spars, polished brass ventilators, a real beauty. We children were over the moon. As a youngster, I watched the large yachts out at sea while standing on a bluff near home. Now, I thought, we could do that. It*

> *was on* Ladybird *that I learned to work as a member of a crew, not always easy when it's family. And to navigate, together with the 101 nuances of sailing a keelboat.* (Adventurer, p. 13)

During the five years that Peter crewed on *Ladybird*, skipper Brian passed on to his son high naval standards of seamanship, maintenance and organisation. They made endless lists and kept meticulous logs. Everything — sails, ropes, gear — had to be constantly checked. Everything, no matter whether cruising or racing, had to be *right*. Even if they were just cruising, they had to go *faster*.

Whether on *Tango* or *Ladybird*, winning was great, but Peter insisted throughout his life that however competitive and tough the sailing was, you also had to have fun. Also, you didn't sail the oceans oblivious of the wildlife. His parents taught him to appreciate the big pods of whales and dolphins sometimes sighted in the Gulf, and how to recognise the many varieties of seabirds. 'We were taught a great awareness of animals,' remembers Tony.

Peter also learned the discipline of living afloat in tiny spaces (not easy for a teenager who was over six foot tall) and respect for his captain's decisions. There were occasions when Peter, and Tony, had to be reminded who was the skipper round here!

As with his three siblings, Peter attended local schools. He went to Bayswater Primary then Belmont Intermediate school, then on to Takapuna Grammar. He recalled that he 'couldn't say I enjoyed school much. I

However competitive, sailing had to be fun! Peter (centre) with brother Tony and sister Liz.

think I spent quite a bit of illegal time drawing boats. And I was too tall.' However, he did what was expected and finished school with a respectable University Entrance pass (now NCEA). He then attended Auckland Technical Institute and gained his New Zealand Certificate in Mechanical Engineering.

However, Peter wasn't much into academic work or team sports like rugby or cricket. Out on the water was where his heart lay and where his real education was happening.

The Hauraki Gulf

The Hauraki Gulf, regarded as one of the world's finest cruising grounds, is enjoyed year-round by many thousands of Aucklanders and visitors. Once out of the Waitemata Harbour, yachts and powerboats can revel in boisterous sea breezes (Hauraki is the Maori word for 'north wind'), or ghost along in light airs with seabirds and dolphins for company. Whales, orca and little blue penguins are also seen.

Great Barrier Island provides shelter from the worst of the Pacific's swells, and the many smaller islands offer safe anchorages and barbecue sites in sandy bays edged with pohutukawa. Swimming is safe, with little to fear from sharks or jellyfish.

It's true that other famous cruising grounds such as the Greek islands or the Caribbean offer more history, warmer climates, picturesque fishing villages and beachside restaurants and bars, but the peaceful, unspoiled nature of the Hauraki Gulf is its chief appeal. Many of the bays and beaches have no houses or shops, or just a few holiday cottages. Crews can drop anchor and choose to be solitary, or enjoy meeting up with other boating families and friends or a spot of fishing.

Two America's Cup regattas held out of Auckland in 1995 and 2000 demonstrated to the world that the inner gulf waters are perfect for racing, providing the powerful Cup boats with challenging winds, comparatively little tide and good spectator viewing. Many world championships for international dinghy classes have been held off North Shore beaches. Year-round, dinghies and keelers can regularly be seen out racing or heading off to quiet outer gulf anchorages.

2

Building boats, learning the ropes

While studying engineering, Peter dreamed of offshore racing. He must have often wondered how he could turn his passion into his job. In early 1960s New Zealand, being a full-time professional crew for racing yachts backed by sponsors was just about unheard of as a career path. Yacht racing, whether keelers or dinghies, was still mostly an amateur pastime.

Peter saw that Waitemata skipper Chris Bouzaid was hitting the headlines in *Rainbow II*, winning the famously tough race between Sydney and Hobart. There was even talk of *Rainbow* being shipped to Germany to take on the Europeans in one of the world's top contests, the One Ton Cup.

Building Bandit *in the family's Bayswater garden.*

About the time he left school, Peter decided to build his own keelboat to race in the Junior Offshore Group (JOG) events run by the Royal Akarana Yacht Club. It was a big call for a teenager, but in those days amateur backyard boat-building was common. Peter had always helped his father with *Ladybird*'s maintenance, meeting Brian's exacting standards.

Helming Ladybird *with brother Tony (left), mother Joyce and sister Liz.*

Peter had also long enjoyed building model yachts using the lines of famous craft like *Britannia* shown in the books of famous British designer, Uffa Fox. He and Tony pored over English magazines such as *Yachting World*, which contained glossy features on successful yachts and their designers.

At 18 he was old enough to make his dream come true. He saved up enough money to send off to *Yachting World* for the plans for a 23-foot (7 metre) plywood keeler by famous Dutch designer, Ricus Van de Stadt, and then, to buy the basic timbers.

Inside a makeshift shed that blocked some of the light into his parents' bedroom, *Bandit* slowly took shape. When not studying or out on *Ladybird* or *Tango*, Peter put in long hours in the shed, often at night. Brother Tony remembers that the little keeler was meticulously and beautifully built.

There was high excitement when it came time to melt the lead to pour the keel. Unfortunately the cast-iron bathtubs set up in the garden for the exercise split apart with the heat. Approximately half a ton of molten lead ran across the crazy paving and into his mother's carefully tended flowerbeds.

Eventually all was in order. The keel was poured, the hull was painted black, the mast was rigged and the sails were stowed. All in time for the champagne launch and the 1967–68 JOG racing season. (There were actually two launches for *Bandit*. In the excitement of the occasion, no one at the Devonport Yacht Club thought to mention that there was insufficient depth for *Bandit* to float off the slipway. She was properly launched the following day.)

With Tony and a close friend as crew, Peter quickly made his mark. On lively downwind legs, rival skippers' yachts got used to the orange and black spinnaker leading the fleet. In *Bandit* Peter won the JOG championship in his very first season as a skipper.

More successes would have followed the next summer except that new design rules meant that *Bandit* was up against bigger and more competitive yachts. Her chances of winning were very much reduced. The solution? Build another boat, one built to the rules!

Peter's shed was resurrected, and he set to work on a 26-footer (7.9 metres) by English designers Holman & Pye. She would be called *Oliver Twist*. However, as the hull and decks neared completion, Peter's heart wasn't fully in it. Perhaps 20-year-old Peter had simply outgrown junior sailing?

Within the Waitemata's close-knit offshore racing community, Peter Blake was becoming known as one of the finest young seamen on the harbour. His years to date on the water in *Japeto*, *Pee Bee*, *Tango*, *Ladybird* and *Bandit*, often in conditions that kept other skippers at home, meant he was already hugely experienced.

With no engine, *Bandit* taught her young skipper some valuable lessons in sail handling. Coming into a mooring or anchorage under sail, whatever the weather,

Bandit *heads out of the Waitemata Harbour.*

requires skill, patience and nerve. On one occasion, following *Ladybird* into an anchorage, *Bandit* ran completely out of wind and took many hours to get into the bay, eventually dropping anchor well after dark.

Racing with the Akarana fleet, *Bandit* was often the smallest boat in the race, and disadvantaged sailing 'on the wind', where waterline length largely determines speed. But her skipper made up for that with his intensely competitive nature and sheer nerve on wild downwind runs. Under her orange and black spinnaker, *Bandit* would often dramatically make up lost ground.

On one occasion, in big seas and starting a downhill leg well back, she stormed through the fleet and arrived at the next mark two miles (3.2 kilometres) ahead.

Bandit *coming into a Hauraki Gulf anchorage.*

While he slogged away at his engineering studies and *Oliver Twist*, Peter was now getting invitations from other skippers to crew on One Ton Cup events and the tough Round North Island race.

His introduction to true ocean racing came in 1969 when he was invited to crew on a 50-foot (15.24 metre) yacht called *Red Feather* for the 1300-mile (2092 kilometre) race between Auckland and Suva (Fiji). Skipper Doug Hazard was a family friend and, like Brian Blake, had served in naval gunboats. One story about that Auckland to Suva race records a frustrated Peter on the helm trying to keep the becalmed boat moving while the rest of the bored crew partied.

That same year Peter was off to sea again, this time with his parents on *Ladybird*. The plan was for Brian, Joyce and Peter to sail to Tonga. Tony and the Blake's younger daughter, Liz, who was still at school, would cruise with them to Fiji and then Peter and his parents would sail *Ladybird* home.

All went according to plan, except for the severe gale that hit *Ladybird* two days north of New Zealand. (Weather forecasting was not nearly as accurate in 1969 as in the current computer and satellite age.) With the little yacht hove to and battened down for around 36 hours, it was Peter's first real experience of a storm at sea and one he said he would never forget. As the foredeck crew, handling the sails as the winds and seas increased, and then later, judging it safe to get *Ladybird* sailing again, even Peter would have found it terrifying.

When *Ladybird* finally sailed back into the Waitemata, Peter was nearly 3000 ocean miles more experienced, not only in heavy weather sailing, but navigation too. Using a sextant to fix a yacht's position was something Peter had regularly practised at home. At night, he would spend hours in the garden with his sextant and a bucket of water, learning and becoming skilled in traditional celestial navigation.

Ladybird *just arrived at a quiet Hauraki Gulf anchorage.*

In later years, he always took his trusty sextant and mathematical tables on board any new boat, no matter what new and fancy navigational systems might be installed. When *Steinlager 2*'s computer went on the blink for two days in the middle of the south Atlantic during his final attempt at the Whitbread Round-the-World trophy, Peter's skill with the sextant kept the boat on the right track.

The art of navigation

The science and art of navigation has developed over more than 2000 years to enable ships' captains to take a vessel safely from one place to another. All standard techniques involve a navigator comparing his boat's current position with known coastlines, islands and other geographical features such as mountain ranges and lighthouses. Until the electronic age, which began nearly 50 years ago, safe navigation was achieved using a number of methods.

Navigators used charts, compasses and, since the 18th century, sextants and numerical tables to establish their position. Day and night officers monitored their ship's progress across an ocean. They mostly used dead reckoning, which uses the ship's course and speed to estimate a position in the future and to avoid hazards. Allowance is made for currents, steering errors and leeway (the sailboat's tendency to slip sideways).

Great explorers such as Columbus, Magellan, Drake, Cabot and Cook used dead reckoning to establish approximate longitude. James Harrison's invention of the marine chronometer in Captain Cook's time allowed mariners to establish precise longitude and thus make ocean navigation considerably more reliable and safe.

Celestial navigation in ancient times used Polaris (the North Star) to determine latitude. Since the 18th century, navigators have used the sextant to observe their positions from the altitude of sun, moon, planets and certain stars to establish a ship's whereabouts on a chart. 'Taking sights' from the deck of a rolling ship or yacht, often with a hazy horizon, was often a tricky exercise.

Today, ships' navigators use sextants only rarely, as back-up to electronic devices that fix a ship's position. These include radio direction-finding systems, and radar to determine distance from known objects such as islands, coastlines, oil rigs and other ships.

Ships and ocean-going yachts mostly rely on satellite navigation, which uses artificial earth satellite systems such as GPS, to determine position. Since the first experimental satellite was launched in 1978, more than 20 GPS satellites have been launched into orbit. These transmit signals back to the receiver, stating location, speed and direction.

As a 21-year-old sailor in the Waitemata of 1969, Peter had served his apprenticeship. Sail-handling, navigation, boat-building, log-keeping, engine maintainence, skippering his own boat or simply being a personable, reliable and respected crew — there wasn't really too much left to learn.

In later years, he always took his trusty sextant and mathematical tables on board any new boat.

To get experience as crew in bigger boats and earn a living in ocean racing he would have to go overseas, probably to Europe. There was a role model. Chris Bouzaid in *Rainbow II* had just stunned the European offshore racing world by winning the famous One Ton Cup. It was no surprise to family or friends when Peter, quite suddenly, decided to abandon his engineering studies, sell the unfinished *Oliver Twist*, and head off on his OE (overseas experience). For an ambitious young sailor, this would mean finding a path into the English sailing scene, where he could become known as a useful crew and hopefully create a job for himself.

Sailing on the Waitemata

When New Zealand won yachting's premier prize, the America's Cup, in 1995, people around the world asked how a tiny country of four and a bit million people could so thoroughly defeat the mighty Americans, 5–0. Later, after Peter Blake led the team that in 2000 won the Cup a second time, they asked how New Zealand could continue to shine in so many top yachting events?

They now know, but did not appreciate then, that famous Kiwi sailors like Chris Bouzaid, Peter Blake, Russell Coutts and Grant Dalton didn't just arrive out of the blue. They belong to an ongoing maritime tradition in Auckland and the Hauraki Gulf that dates back to well before the first days of European settlement in 1840.

In pre-European times, Maori in their carved waka were

traditionally skilled mariners and fishermen. After the arrival of Pakeha, by the 1850s vessels under sail owned by Maori and settlers alike were trading up and down the coast.

From the 1880s fine yachts designed by famous boat-builders such as the Logan family and Charles Bailey were appearing on the harbour. After another 50 years of steady growth, and in late 1930s, sailors from the Waitemata started winning events all over the world: in Europe, America, Australia, at England's famous Cowes Week and at the Olympic Games.

They won in international dinghy classes, the new boardsailing class, in comparatively small keelers, right up to the powerful America's Cup and Whitbread (later Volvo) Round-the-World boats.

Funding came from wealthy corporate sponsors who wanted to promote New Zealand overseas. Designers, boat-builders and sail-makers contributed to Auckland's internationally-recognised maritime industry. Crews were and still are drawn from amateur clubs that for more than a century have held races in the Gulf's changeable conditions, nurturing a breed of tough, resilient sailors second to none.

3

'Sea Fever' and twice around the world

'There comes a time,' Peter wrote many years later, 'when no matter how many small boats you build or how many inshore races you compete in, Sea Fever calls you out on to the deep oceans, the lonely sea and the sky.' (*Adventurer*, p. 18)

His timing was pretty good. The sport of offshore racing was gathering momentum in Britain and Europe, and there was much excitement about the first Whitbread Round-the-World race planned for 1973–74.

Little did Peter know then that over the next 17 years he would do this race five times. Winning it in his own boat, designed, built and sailed by New Zealanders, would become close to an obsession.

But first he had to establish himself as a useful crew. By great good luck, or perhaps some shrewd foresight, in Malta he introduced himself to a famous British yachtsman, Les Williams. Williams was preparing his 70-foot (21.3 metre) ketch *Ocean Spirit*, another Van de Stadt design, for the first race across the southern Atlantic, from Cape Town to Rio de Janeiro. The tall Kiwi impressed Les Williams as pleasant, polite and willing to work. He was fit and strong. 'And he knew a bit about sailing.'

Within days, Peter was invited to join *Ocean Spirit* for the delivery voyage to Cape Town, and then, as a watch leader, on the 3500-mile (4828 kilometre) race itself. Co-owner Robin

Rounding the famous Fastnet rock off Ireland's southernmost tip.

Knox-Johnson, another important figure in Peter's story, was equally impressed. Knox-Johnson wrote that Peter, 'was one of the youngest on board but he had authority, knew what he was doing and his watch very quickly respected him. He was also good to deal with — a guy you dragged into the consultations because he'd got good views to give.'

From greenhorn crew to watch leader to … skipper? After *Ocean Spirit* finished first in Rio de Janeiro and both owners flew back to London, it was 22-year-old Peter who Williams asked to deliver the maxi-yacht back to England. Not bad for the boy from Bayswater whose sole command to date had been a 23-foot plywood boat he built himself!

With *Ocean Spirit* safely delivered, Peter returned to Auckland, where he got a job with Yachtspars, a company that manufactured masts. He also navigated a top one-tonner called *Escapade* on the 1973 Auckland to Suva race. When Les Williams wrote from England asking Peter to join the crew of his new 80-footer (24.3 metre) *Burton Cutter* for the Whitbread race due to start in September of that year, he was off like a shot.

The first Whitbread race was challenging for all concerned. Seventeen boats from seven nations took eight months to race from Portsmouth to Cape Town to Sydney to Rio de Janeiro and back to Portsmouth. On the way three crewmen were lost overboard and many others were injured. In extreme conditions several yachts were stripped of their masts and spinnakers. Others suffered near-disastrous knock-downs and broaches; at least one was pitchpoled. Most were significantly damaged in some way.

Burton Cutter's campaign went from dodgy to bad to worse. She was expected to be fast, but she started unprepared. Food boxes arrived at the eleventh hour and had to be stored in makeshift nets. The toilet overflowed. The decks, not yet caulked, leaked on to crew in the unfinished bunks below. (One had to sleep under a big black umbrella.) The thrill of arriving first to a hero's welcome in Cape Town gave way to despair. Early on the second leg to Sydney it was discovered that *Burton Cutter* had been structurally damaged by weeks of hard close-hauled sailing.

> *The thrill of arriving first to a hero's welcome in Cape Town gave way to despair.*

The southern ocean is no place to be in a full gale with a boat that is beginning to break up. Skipper Williams decided to turn back to Port Elizabeth in South Africa. Peter found himself placed in charge of an 80-foot racing maxi for her extensive repairs and then the long passage from South Africa to rejoin the Whitbread fleet in Rio for the final leg across the Atlantic.

Peter was promoted quickly, wrote Les Williams, 'because he deserved it ... I could trust him implicitly and that's a wonderful feeling — you can go to sleep and know everything is in very good hands.'

Burton Cutter ended the Whitbread on a high, coming second into Portsmouth. It had been a fantastic eight months.

Typically, Peter wrote in his personal log that the hardships were overshadowed by the hospitality extended in the ports and friendships made among sailors from 14 countries.

What on earth could he do that would not seem too dull or boring after such an adventure?

The answer was another hazardous race with Les Williams in *Burton Cutter* — but with only two crew instead of 14. The 1974 Two-man Round Britain race would take a motley collection of 67 boats, both monohulls and multihulls, clockwise round Britain and Ireland. Williams and Blake in *Burton Cutter* finished the gruelling 1900-mile (3057 kilometre) event in not quite 20 days and well ahead of all the conventional monohulls. The faster speeds of even the smaller multihulls, however, had left Peter with food for thought. He might be tempted, he mused, by the offer of a large racing trimaran.

For the moment he'd had enough of yacht racing. Possibly he was still uncertain, even after his exploits on *Burton Cutter*, whether offshore racing could become a career. He decided, now that he'd 'grown up', to return to New Zealand and look to finding 'a proper career'. The problem was then, and still was (he wrote 20 years later) that, 'I still don't know the answer to that.'

So, he went back to Auckland for something completely different: a private pilot's licence, a lot of diving and cruising around the active volcano of White Island and a job as an industrial sales engineer.

The sea continued to call. In 1975 he raced with friends from Auckland to Gisborne, from Sydney to Hobart, from Hobart to Auckland.

Adventure further afield beckoned. He became skipper and engineer on a luxury 72-foot (21.9 metre) motor yacht called *Dina* belonging to a wealthy Arab. Sailing around the eastern Mediterranean was a cruisy job and no doubt, very well paid. His crew were Arab and were 'pretty hopeless sailors so I had to learn to yell at them in Arabic.'

It was also dangerous. In one incident he had to leap to *Dina*'s controls and roar out of the marina in war-torn Beirut bound for Cyrpus, with the owner's two sons aboard and close behind, the sounds of machine-gun fire. 'Great fun,' he could later write.

However, ocean racing was still the life he longed for. When Les Williams asked him to join the next Whitbread race on *Heath's Condor*, Peter accepted 'with indecent haste.'

His role would be an unusual one. Les Williams and Robin Knox-Johnston would share the skippering; Peter would be the steady, dependable first mate for the whole campaign, providing continuity. In effect, he was the 'head honcho.'

All his skills and resources were tested. Major design problems on the 77-foot (23.4 metre) maxi were identified even before the start from Portsmouth. Weakened by severe squalls on the first leg to Cape Town, the carbon fibre mast (then new and untried technology) snapped in two. A replacement alloy mast was flown to Monrovia, halfway down Africa's western coast. By the time it was fitted the Whitbread fleet was 12 days ahead. Any chance of overall honours for *Heath's Condor* was gone.

She continued on with the race. Peter marvelled at the beauty and danger of the Southern Ocean: the icebergs, soaring albatrosses and the glorious night skies; also the dangers to a maxi yacht charging along at high speed posed by gale-force westerlies, raging seas, the submerged remains of icebergs and -10°C temperatures at night.

> ... *your compass goes haywire, whales appear from nowhere, and worst of all are the growlers that lurk beneath the surface. These are pieces of iceberg big enough to slice the yacht open. You are cold and damp for days on end, and get very little sleep. But it is also like going to the dentist: marvellous when it's over.*
> (Adventurer, p. 24)

They nearly lost a crewman when he was flipped overboard by a sail. Fortunately he caught the life-ring tossed to him; even more fortunately a circling flock of albatross (perhaps thinking he was edible) marked his position until *Heath's Condor* could work back through the raging seas to pull him safely aboard.

The arrival of the first Whitbread fleet to call at Auckland was spectacular. With *Heath's Condor* first over the line, and all the crew dressed in 'whites' as smart as any warship coming in to port, media and public alike wanted to know more about the local boy who was the winner's sailing master. The fleet's departure, amidst literally thousands of boats and spectators onshore, was an epic spectacle. It was the type of farewell for which the Waitemata has become famous.

He might be tempted, he mused, by the offer of a large racing trimaran.

The remaining two legs passed without major incident for *Heath's Condor*. She arrived second in Rio, and satisfactorily first across the line in Portsmouth. It had been another race of mixed fortunes: enough exhilarating racing and line honours for individual legs but mechanical failures denying the owners and Peter the reward of a better overall result. Even so, Peter remembered *Heath's Condor* as 'a truly beautiful yacht, one of the nicest that it has ever been my fortune to sail on. No matter what the weather she was well-mannered.'

With two Whitbreads, the Cape Town to Rio, the Round Britain and a number of Pacific long-distance events under his belt, at 29 years of age, Peter was now one of the world's more experienced offshore yachtsmen. The two Whitbread campaigns had provided invaluable lessons. He'd sailed through gales and calms with two of Britain's most famous and respected long-distance sailors, but he now knew a good deal about the challenges and pitfalls of sponsored maxi racing, both at sea and on shore.

It was time to branch out, to spread his wings. The next Whitbread, he decided, would be on a New Zealand boat.

Round-the-world sailing

During the 20th century, with nearly all commercial ships now using the Suez and Panama canals, there has been a revival of sailing in the Southern Ocean. Today's southern seafarers are recreational and racing blue-water yachts, setting records for sailing solo or two-man or fully crewed, with one, two or no stops, via Cape Horn, with or against the prevailing winds. In recent years there have also been attempts by teenagers to be the youngest, although worldwide controversy has resulted in 'youngest' claims no longer being officially recognised.

In 1895, American captain Joshua Slocum was the first to sail single-handed around the world, although it's thought he took an inshore route through the islands and not south of the Horn proper. His 37-foot (11 metre) sloop, *Spray*, a rebuilt oyster dredger, took more than three years to complete the journey. Maybe then, it was the 42-foot (13 metre) yacht *Saoirse,* sailed by Irish adventurer Conor O'Brien and three crew, that was the first small boat to circumnavigate the world via Cape Horn in 1924.

In 1966, Sir Frances Chichester, at 64, became the first to sail solo around the world with only one stop in his 53-foot (16 metre) ketch, *Gypsy Moth IV.*

One of the few to complete the voyage against the prevailing winds was Chay Blyth in his ketch *British Steel.* He achieved this in 1971, taking 302 days. Two years later, Frenchman Alain Colas, aboard his trimaran *Manureva*, took 129 days.

The first woman to sail solo around the world was Polish-born Krystyna Chojnowska-Liskiewicz. Her journey starting in 1976, from and back to the Canary Islands, took 401 days. New Zealand-born Dame Naomi James was the first woman to sail single-handed around the world via Cape Horn's classic clipper route. She left Dartmouth in September 1977 and returned in June 1978. Her 272-day passage in the 53-foot (16 metre) yacht *Express Crusader* beat Sir Francis Chichester's record by two days.

In 1998 Australian Kay Cottee became the first woman to complete a non-stop single-handed circumnavigation on *Blackmore's First Lady*. Her voyage took 189 days. Eleven years later British yachtswoman Dee Caffari became the first woman to sail solo, non-stop both ways around the world. In May 2006 she had completed her 'wrong way' voyage (against the prevailing winds and currents), taking 178 days in a 72-foot steel yacht. Three years later Caffari took less than 100 days to complete her circumnavigation the 'right' way around the world.

During the 1980s Australian Jon Sanders set a number of remarkable records including first to circumnavigate Antarctica, first single-handed sailor to remain continuously at sea twice around the world, longest distance continuously sailed by any yacht (48,510 miles or 78,070 kilometres) and the longest period alone at sea during a continuous voyage, not quite 420 days. In 1986 he completed three solo non-stop circumnavigations aboard his 47-foot (14 metre) yacht *Parry Endeavour*.

Famous young sailors include English-born Michael Perham. In August 2009, at 17 years of age, he became the youngest person to sail around the world solo in his 50-footer (15.24 metre) *totallymoney.com*, beating the record set only six weeks earlier by Zac Sunderland, a 17-year-old American. Another is Australian Jessica Watson, 16, whose yacht, *Ella's Pink Lady* took her around both capes (with several stops) in 210 days, setting an unofficial 'youngest' record.

As well as sailors seeking achievement and records, there are today several major round-the-world races via Cape Horn. The first was the single-handed *Sunday Times* Golden Globe Race (won by Robin Knox-Johnston), which led to the present-day Around Alone race, which allows stops, and the Vendée Globe, which is non-stop. Both are single-handed races held every four years. Previously called the Whitbread, the Volvo Ocean Race is a crewed race with stops and is also sailed every four years. The Trophée Jules Verne is a prize for the fastest circumnavigation of the world by any type of yacht, with no restrictions on the size of the crew, no assistance and non-stop.

4

Ceramco: 'The Porcelain Rocket Ship'

In 1977, *Heath's Condor* had not been Peter's ideal option for his second Whitbread.

If the plans he and his Devonport Yacht Club mate Martin Foster dreamed up during 1975 had actually worked out, Peter would have sailed a New Zealand maxi in the race. Their entry, a boat that would sail fast downwind, would have been designed by a young and exciting Auckland designer called Bruce Farr. The campaign would be publicly promoted by Peter Mulgrew, a famous New Zealand adventurer, and sponsored, they hoped, by Air New Zealand.

Sadly, Air New Zealand declined, seeing 'no advantage whatsoever' in being associated with a yachting project. The first Whitbread had put into Sydney, not Auckland, so Kiwi companies hadn't seen for themselves how big the event could be; or, as Peter put it, 'the merit of pouring a lot of money into a young man's pipedream.'

Out of time to find another Whitbread sponsor, Peter and Martin persuaded the Devonport Yacht Club to run a Two-man Round North Island race, without relying on sponsors. The 1200-mile (1931 kilometre) race, no less challenging than the Round Britain, was planned to coincide with the bicentenary of Captain Cook's third voyage to New Zealand. The success of the first race helped make it a regular event on the Auckland yachting calendar. Prince Philip, with Queen Elizabeth watching, fired the starting gun for the 44 entries assembled off the Devonport Wharf. It was no surprise to anyone when Peter and Graham Eder sailed their 42-foot (12.8 metre) *Gerontius* first across the line.

Not long after, Peter was off to *Heath's Condor* and his second Whitbread. After the race he was committed to her new owner Bob Bell to skipper several major offshore events and eventually deliver *Condor of Bermuda* (her new name) to Sydney and finally Auckland. As straightforward as it sounded, Peter's life was about to get rather more complicated.

He was still working with Martin Foster on plans for a New Zealand entry for the third Whitbread in 1981. What he had not expected while supervising *Condor*'s repairs at a boatyard in Emsworth, on England's southern coast, was to fall in love. Visiting the local sailing club one Friday night he met 'this slim blonde girl who I thought was rather pretty.' He and Pippa Glanville, he soon discovered, shared a love of the sea and a taste for having fun: 'We were able to laugh at the same things.'

Pippa, for her part, was 'literally smitten' by the tall blond Kiwi. 'Wow!' It was, she would later admit, love at first sight, which seemed to be mutual. She recalls there seemed to be an aura surrounding him, something in his eyes. 'He often had that far-away look like when he was at sea; you could see him scanning the horizon, but he wasn't just looking at the horizon, he was looking yonder.'

Peter left on *Condor* as planned, but by this time he'd asked Pippa to be on the dockside to say goodbye, and then, the day before leaving, to join him in the Caribbean. Nothing as exciting had ever happened to her before. Peter had also (perhaps shrewdly) invited her brother Charles to join the delivery crew. So, shortly after Christmas 1978, Pippa flew to the Caribbean and found herself an unofficial crew member, racing on *Condor* from Nassau to Miami. It was a tough overnight race in huge waves and strong headwinds, which they passed eating roast beef sandwiches and getting through a bottle of port.

Perhaps, she thought, she had passed Peter's sailing test, for very soon after, in Miami, in *Condor*'s aft cabin, Peter proposed. It was all quite formal. He didn't want to rush her. She could have time to think about it. But Pippa, 'overjoyed at the thought of joining Peter on a huge adventure,' didn't need time. She was so happy to be part of his life, the immediate answer without reservation was 'Yes!'

> He met 'this slim blonde girl who I thought was rather pretty.'

Pippa was further tested when she was appointed cook on her first official ocean race on *Condor* with Peter, from Miami to Montego Bay in Jamaica. Seventeen big guys needed a lot of food, and having to cook strapped upright in the galley wasn't much fun. Her pleas to the skipper after the race to do anything, *anything* on the boat except cook, were heeded. From then on she sailed as deck crew, relishing Peter's new world of global sailing.

Peter's life, always busy, got busier. He had an upcoming wedding and was in ongoing talks with Martin Foster for the 1981 Whitbread challenge. He had to return *Condor* to Britain for the classic biennial race from Cowes to the Fastnet Rock south of Ireland and back to Plymouth. The wedding would take place a week later.

Peter won widespread praise for skippering *Condor* with great skill and nerve to win the Fastnet race, finishing first and breaking the race record held by her American archrival *Kialoa III*. It was a hair-raising ride across the Irish Sea, even by Peter's standards. *Condor* was knocked flat more than once in seas worse than the southern oceans. In the last stages of the race, through driving rain and bad visibility, Peter had her going under spinnaker at 20 knots or more. However, on arrival nobody was celebrating and the result was almost forgotten as the race hit world headlines for all the wrong reasons.

Of the 303 boats that entered, only 85 completed the course. All but one of the 14 maxis had been ahead of the real blow, too far in front to help boats in trouble other than relay messages. The rest, mostly the smaller yachts, withdrew, intent on saving their yachts and their lives as a severe, unexpected Atlantic storm, force 10 or more, overwhelmed the fleet. Five yachts were 'lost believed sunk', and another 15 were abandoned but later recovered. Rescuers in helicopters, lifeboats, merchant and naval ships saved some 136 people, but 15 died at sea. It was and remains the most disastrous Fastnet on record.

Little wonder that Pippa Glanville, driving down to Plymouth and hearing the tragedy unfold on the car radio, was desperate to know that *Condor*, with both her fiance and her brother on board, had safely arrived. There would, happily, be a wedding and a short honeymoon in Scotland. Then they would be making preparations for a long delivery voyage to Sydney and on to Auckland. 'We didn't own a house,' wrote Pippa. 'Peter wasn't on a salary and we didn't own anything as such. Nor did it matter … my parents were apprehensive, but they had great confidence in Peter. They could see he was strong and very charismatic and would protect their daughter.'

With food supplies aboard *Condor* for eight people for 100 days, and six rifles in case of pirates in the Red Sea, the newlyweds set off on an idyllic 'second honeymoon' through Gibraltar and on to

Wedding day in Emsworth, August 1979.

Port Said, Jeddah, Danger Island and Diego Garcia in the Indian Ocean, Perth and Sydney.

They did the Sydney to Hobart race together, then weathered a cyclone en route to New Zealand. Imagine *Condor* hove to for 24 hours in mammoth waves, Peter and his new wife on their two-hour watch, 'strapped in the cockpit, crouched low, with huge waves breaking over us, and the wheel lashed hard over.' It was clear that Peter had chosen his life partner well: no stay-at-home wife, she would become his 'right-hand man' for all his yachting activities right up until the America's Cup.

In Auckland Peter's commitment to *Condor* came to an end. He was now free to concentrate on the Whitbread campaign, which was gathering momentum. The campaign had been publicly announced, resulting in the Royal New Zealand Yacht Squadron joining the Devonport Yacht Club as official supporters. Bruce Farr had again been approached as designer of the sort of boat, a somewhat smaller maxi, that Peter felt had a chance of winning. 'We wanted a fair, fast hull — a boat which could maintain high speeds readily and stay with the weather systems for longer without exhausting the crew.'

Martin Foster had found a probable major sponsor in leading businessman Tom Clark. It took only one meeting with Peter for Tom Clark to be convinced that a New Zealand Whitbread campaign would raise the profile of his ceramics company, Ceramco, and 'do something to give the country a bit of a psychological uplift.' A win was certainly possible.

Tom Clark was no stranger to offshore racing; his yacht *Buccaneer* had taken line honours in the 1970 Sydney to Hobart race. He understood boats and as a successful businessman he knew about leadership. So, Ceramco Company provided most of the funds. For the rest, the public was offered the chance to express their support with $500 shares. More than 600 companies and individuals responded enthusiastically. Little New Zealand's entry in the mighty Whitbread would appear in

Peter and his crew on board Ceramco.

the media and public's imagination as very much 'the people's boat.'

By October 1981 the 68-foot (17.67 metre) aluminium *Ceramco New Zealand*, now fondly known as The Porcelain Rocketship, was ready to be launched with full pomp and ceremony by the Governor-General's wife, Dame Norma Holyoake. The crew of *Steinlager 2* had been chosen. Not just by interviews; Peter decided on the unusual strategy of taking 18 out of 140 applicants on a rugged three-day tramp around Lake Waikaremoana. Pippa went too, determined to keep up.

Rather than simply choose the most experienced, Peter chose 11 good sailors but specially those that he thought would get on well together for nine months in cramped and testing conditions. Among them were a doctor, a lawyer, a bookseller, a plumber, an electrician, a concrete contractor and two teachers. It was to be a characteristic of nearly all of Peter's crews in the years ahead: they would become and would remain close and loyal friends.

One who made the last 18 but not the final crew was a notably tough and resourceful 23-year old by the name of Grant Dalton. Missing out, he would say later, was, 'to this day, absolutely crushing', but he went on, with Peter's indirect help, to sail the Whitbread on the leading Dutch maxi *Flyer*. Later he would sail with Peter on *Lion New Zealand* and with his own boat, *Fisher & Paykel*, pose a serious threat to Peter's hopes of Whitbread success in *Steinlager 2*. Eventually he would become CEO for Team New Zealand.

One whose place in Peter's crew was challenged was his wife. Tom Clark wasn't used to women on racing boats and announced that if she was on board for the passage to Sydney and the race to Hobart, he would not be.

Peter replied that either Pippa was on board, 'or I won't be there on the boat and for the race as skipper, or indeed, at all.'

In the end Pippa and Tom, recognising that Peter meant what he said, both sailed across the Tasman and on the Hobart race. It took one 'atrocious' broach just north of Auckland and a nasty storm north of Cape Reinga for Tom Clark to see that Pippa may be a slim and attractive woman, but she was a fully competent and experienced crew. As Tom Clark was already a firm friend and mentor to Peter, he would also become a lifelong friend to Pippa.

Yachting commentator Peter Montgomery took this spectacular shot of Peter, wearing safety harness, at the helm of Ceramco.

> ## Why are there handicaps in yacht racing?
>
> Dinghies like P-class and Optimists, Olympic designs like Lasers and the maxis used in the America's Cup are raced in classes. In 'Class' racing all hull designs, sails, rigging and gear are covered by strict rules so that the boats are identical or very similar. These rules ensure that competition between crews is fair.
>
> For races where the entries include boats of different lengths and designs, handicap systems are used to allow one boat to race as fairly as possible against another. Otherwise, longer, lighter (and more expensive) boats would theoretically always be faster and have the advantage.
>
> For handicap races like the Whitbread, each boat is given a rating. This depends on individual features such as the design of the hull and keel, the sail plan, modifications to the rig and type of rudder and propeller.
>
> This rating number then allows race officials to adjust the final results to reflect the greatest achievement of actual seamanship: good navigation, the course chosen, the excellence and courage of the crew work.
>
> Handicap races have two winners: the first to finish taking 'line honours', and the handicap winner. When a yacht takes a line and handicap double, that is recognised as a significant accomplishment.

In December 1980, *Ceramco New Zealand* was ready to take on the world. Her first race was the 630-mile (1013 kilometre) Sydney to Hobart race, where she proved her speed by finishing first, with the second boat nearly two hours behind.

Not only that, she emerged handicap winner as well: a double winner on her first outing and only the third time in the race's history that a double win had been achieved. Peter was elated. He wrote, 'The boat performed 'like it was on rails ... we found that *Ceramco* would flat run just like a big dinghy, lifting her bow out and riding on top of the seas as straight as an arrow. No control problems and no broaches — just the characteristics we wanted for the Southern Ocean.'

There was no resting on laurels. Early in the New Year Peter took *Ceramco* south to give his crew a taste of surfing a maxi downwind through high seas and at high speed — they experienced three spectacular broaches and one knockdown — before heading back for a promotional tour around New Zealand.

'If Blake's XI had any doubts as to what they were involved in, they were gone now,' wrote Peter after their grand Waitemata welcome and a good deal of national media attention. '*Ceramco* and her crew were celebrities. We'd won respect and silenced the critics.'

The young man's pipedream was a reality.

With time running short, *Ceramco* was shipped to Philadelphia, accompanied by Peter and Pippa, and sailed by them and a crew on to England. Some preliminary races around the Solent during Cowes Week convinced Peter that the Dutch *Flyer* would be the boat to beat.

As the day of the Whitbread start approached, Peter had to tell Pippa she would not be in the crew. Bluntly, she didn't have the big-boat experience, nor the sheer strength when things got really tough. Though 'bitterly disappointed', Pippa acknowledged the logic and sense of his decision, waved them off happily and enjoyed staying connected to Peter and the race by frequent radio contact.

All went according to plan with the start off Portsmouth. *Flyer* and *Ceramco* led the fleet out into the English Channel and paced each other for the next 22 days. With a powerful radio on board, Peter spent a good deal of time keeping sponsors and the public, via radio stations and print journalists, fully informed. Through the Equator, into the south Atlantic and a little north of Ascension Island, *Ceramco* was 'going like a rocket.'

On the twenty-third day, Pippa's call from Peter was catastrophic. His log read: 'September 21, 1981. 12.35 hours. Mast came down — **** it.' With the gun-fire crack of the breaking mast, any chance of winning the leg towards overall success in his third Whitbread was gone.

It wasn't the mast that failed, as some armchair critics in Auckland had feared. 'We could have been using a telephone pole ... it was a rigging failure,' Peter insisted. One of the fittings on the spreaders had gone, leaving the mast insufficiently supported. Bobbing around like a cork on the ocean, feeling utterly alone and distressed that they'd let down their country, the men on *Ceramco* had about 2500 miles (4023 kilometres) to go to Cape Town.

Disaster on board Ceramco.

'But it was no good calling for Mum,' Peter wrote. First, the crew must swiftly pull the broken mast and a mess of sail and rigging back on board before any of it punched a hole in the hull. Then, he considered his options. He could head back to Monrovia (shades of *Condor*), or even more unthinkable, motor on (but put himself out of the race) to Cape Town. Or, they could continue to race.

Peter made a decision that is today legendary in the history of long-distance sailing. As he remembered it, 'twenty-four hours later, under jury rig and with three million New Zealanders glued to their radios, we were sailing again, covering 200 miles [320 kilometres] a day.' It was a spectacular feat of seamanship, confidence and sheer nerve. The crew rigged *Ceramco* as the most bizarre ketch ever seen on the seven seas. Peter chose a longer downwind route (1000 miles or 1609 kilometres longer) to get more favourable winds, as the clipper ships had once done.

Although they looked 'a bit like a Chinese laundry,' *Ceramco* made steady progress, at times reaching 11 knots. At one point they had to reef the jury rig! Peter allowed no brooding. If anyone wanted to get demoralised, he told them to 'come and see me and we'll get demoralised together.'

After three and a half weeks under jury rig, they were the last boat to arrive in to Cape Town, 11 days behind *Flyer*, but their sporting courage was warmly applauded. Pippa, who'd been in Cape Town helping as shore crew, watched their approach from a small plane.

Now the Kiwi team had just over two weeks to step the $150,000 replacement mast flown (in three pieces) from Auckland, and generally prepare *Ceramco* for the mighty southern oceans. There wasn't time for dreaming about what might have been. Peter later wrote, 'I wasn't gutted at all. I honestly wasn't. If you do enough sailing, you realise these things happen. Sometimes they're within your control, sometimes they aren't. You have to put up with it …'

He was, however, very concerned about the good faith and money that had been invested in *Ceramco* by her backers and the New Zealand public. Determined to show how good *Ceramco* could be, the crew almost forgot about the overall prize. 'We knew we weren't going to win that, so we set out to win as many of the other legs as we possibly could.' Even with an untried mast and a slightly apprehensive crew, *Ceramco* charged through the wild southern oceans, neck and neck with *Flyer* for most of the passage.

Peter's dream of sailing first into Auckland was not to be. Finding more favourable winds in the Tasman, *Flyer* rounded Waitemata's North Head eight hours ahead. But second out of 26 was more than respectable, and *Ceramco* won the leg on handicap.

It was a similar story on the third leg to Mar del Plata, on Argentina's coast, and the final leg back up the Atlantic to Portsmouth. *Flyer* was first home, with *Ceramco* close behind, again taking handicap honours.

Overall, despite sailing 3000 miles (4828 kilometres) under jury rig, *Ceramco* was third fastest round the world. She was also the winner of the Roaring Forties Trophy for the best handicap performance from Cape Town to Auckland to Mar del Plata. *Ceramco* was designed and built for the conditions and under extreme hardship she had excelled herself.

Peter could be happy that he'd kept faith with his backers and the fascinated public. He wrote '… both *Flyer* and *Ceramco* were pushed to the limit in a manner none of us will ever forget. We set new standards for big ocean racers. The Whitbread race will be the better and more exciting for it.' He believed that it said a lot about character and commitment that *Flyer* and *Ceramco* were the only two boats to do the entire race without a single change of crew.

Would he have another crack at that elusive Whitbread prize? Try yet again after three races where the first boat broke up around him and the next two suffered tragic dismastings on what were potential winners? Hadn't he frequently said publicly that his third Whitbread would be his last? At 35, he was saying, perhaps rather unconvincingly, he had to settle down, particularly as he and Pippa wanted children. However, almost in the next

Spirit of New Zealand *takes teenagers to sea to learn leadership and team-building skills.*

breath he said, 'there lingers this feeling of unfinished business ... the temptation will be there ...' The third Whitbread finished at the end of March 1982. The crew had gone their separate ways, and *Ceramco* was for sale.

In August, travelling the country by road, Peter was lending his high public profile to the Spirit of Adventure Trust to raise funds for a $6 million tall ship to take young people to sea for leadership training. (That ship, the three-masted *Spirit of New Zealand*, would be one of the course markers for the successful 2000 defence of the America's Cup.)

It seemed 1982 was turning out to be a more relaxed, even a domestic year for the Blakes at the home they were making in the quiet English village of Emsworth, suitable for their first child due in May 1983.

It came as no surprise to people in the international yachting community to hear the rumour that, despite any talk of settling down, Peter had been deliberating for some time with Tom Clark and potential designers about his next Whitbread boat. Or that he'd been to Buckingham Palace, elegant in a hired grey morning suit, to receive an MBE from the Queen for services to sailing.

Peter and Pippa outside Buckingham Palace, on their way to receive an MBE from Queen Elizabeth.

The Southern Ocean

The Southern Ocean is the fourth largest of the world's great oceans (the Arctic is the fifth). Completely surrounding Antarctica, it takes in the southern portions of the Atlantic, Indian and Pacific oceans, generally defined as from latitude 60° south. This southern ocean zone is where cold, northward flowing waters from the Antarctic mix with warmer sub-Antarctic waters. The Antarctic Circumpolar Current moves eastwards, carrying a hundred times greater flow than all the world's rivers. Winds blow unceasingly from the west. The sea temperature varies from -2°C to 10°C.

Since the great European explorers of the 16th century – sailors such as Francisco de Hoces, Ferdinand Magellan and Sir Francis Drake, and (some believe) early Chinese fleets – the unrestricted sea conditions of the southern ocean have posed fearsome challenges to seafarers.

For centuries the world's trade was carried out by sailing ships on eastbound passages around the southern tip of Africa (Cape of Good Hope) or South America (Cape Horn). All the Southern Ocean is wild, cold and desolate, but nowhere is more notorious than the seas around Cape Horn. There, the unrestricted flow of immensely deep water must squeeze through a shallower 600-mile (965-kilometre) gap between the tip of South America and the Antarctic peninsula of Graham Land. In the Drake Passage, the seas accelerate, becoming steeper and more hazardous to tall ships and, in the last hundred years, to yachts.

The opening of the Suez Canal in 1869 and the Panama Canal in 1914 resulted in little use of the southern oceans by trading vessels. Today the southern oceans are used by ships taking tourists to the Antarctic Peninsula or the Ross Sea or by blue water yachts.

The optimum time for rounding the Cape is in the summer months, November to March, of course east about (eastwards). The experience of Captain William Bligh, who tried to take *Bounty* west-about as a short cut to Tahiti in 1787 was instructive to other captains; after three months of horrendous conditions trying to get through the Drake Passage, he gave up and went the long way round.

5

Lion New Zealand: 'The Urban Assault Vehicle'

*L*ion *New Zealand* was a handsome 78-foot (23.7 metre) maxi, but she was not the boat that most observers expected Peter to build for his fourth Whitbread. He'd been very clear about his preference for a typical Bruce Farr design: light displacement, fast on the long downwind legs but still competitive upwind, and crucially, capable of being pushed hard with a small crew.

After the success of his first, bigger boat, *Ceramco*, Bruce Farr was regarded as one of the world's most exciting designers (he would later move from Auckland to a successful career based in America, near Annapolis, Maryland.)

Why did Peter go with a much heavier and larger maxi from another leading designer, Ron Holland, a Kiwi who'd made his home and his name in Cork, Ireland? There were good reasons. Peter, and his faithful supporter Tom Clark, had carefully noted the Whitbread winning performance of the bigger *Flyer*. The two stars of the current maxi scene, *Kialoa IV* and *Condor 2*, had been designed by Ron Holland. Peter had let it be known that he wanted a boat with an unbreakable, heavy-duty hull and a mast and rig that wouldn't let him down. His ideal would combine the radical virtues of a Farr *Ceramco* and a more conservative Holland maxi.

The result was *Lion New Zealand*, so named because another major sponsor had entered the picture. Unlike Tom Clark,

Douglas Myers wasn't a yachtsman. His interest in enabling Peter to enter his fourth Whitbread was commercial and patriotic. He saw Peter as 'something special', a potential winner, and he wanted his brewery company and New Zealand to be associated with success.

The day that *Lion's* metallic silver hull was launched in Auckland, on 4 November 1984, Peter knew in his heart that Whitbread success was going to be hard won, even unlikely. She floated beautifully, but just too deeply in the water. With her extra-strong hull, mast and rig still to go in and two tons more lead in the keel than stipulated in the original design, *Lion* was simply going to be too heavy to be competitive. In yachting terms, she was overbuilt. Privately, Peter was deeply concerned, talking endlessly with the designer and builders for ways to reduce the weight. Publicly, he was all confidence.

He hand-picked the 22 crew necessary to sail the bigger boat, one of them a 26-year-old watch captain named Grant Dalton. They sailed *Lion* to Sydney, eager to see how she would perform against other maxis in the classic race to Hobart. The weather was apalling. While not as disastrous for the fleet as the Fastnet four years earlier, it was the worst Sydney to Hobart race on record. In gale force southwesterlies, one crewman was lost and others were seriously injured. Of 152 boats, many turned back seriously damaged and only 46 finished in Hobart.

Peter's confidence in *Lion* seemed fully justified: she ploughed through huge seas in headwinds of 40 knots, not only staying in the race but easily beating the opposition.

Keen New Zealand listeners had been able to follow the race as it happened. An extra man on board *Lion* was radio commentator Peter Montgomery (whose distinctive voice became famous during the America's Cup years). Montgomery described going through the gale like 'driving a 10-ton truck off the top of a three-storey building every couple of minutes.' No

Lion New Zealand *being escorted by a huge spectator fleet while leaving Auckland for the fourth Whitbread Round-the-World race.*

wonder *Lion* became known, perhaps pointedly, as 'The Urban Assault Vehicle'.

To the New Zealand public, however, she was Peter Blake's glamorous new maxi, the people's boat with the immaculate pedigree that was going to help him win Whitbread glory in the northern hemisphere. Finally!

Peter and the crew began a promotional tour of New Zealand, beginning at Milford and Bluff. There were to be 14 ports of call. However, this tour was on a different scale compared to that undertaken in *Ceramco*. In sun and rain, more than 40,000 people queued for hours for the chance to buy *Lion* merchandise and inspect the boat. The enthusiasm shown in every one of the ports visited was extraordinary, the hospitality almost overwhelming. Promotional work was tough on the crew, but as Peter said, 'in the tougher months to come, maybe in the middle of a bad night in the Southern Ocean, they would remember the little old ladies from the country areas of New Zealand who travelled far and handed over hard-earned dollars to see what those young fellas from Auckland were up to this time and to do their bit to help.'

First, though, they had to get *Lion* to England. Shipping was costly, so the decision was made to sail via the Panama Canal. The delivery crew of five heard that also on board would be Pippa and baby Sarah-Jane, coming up to her second birthday. For family man Peter this was perfectly natural; where he went, Pippa and offspring went too. Seven hundred disposable nappies, a washing machine, dress-ups for King Neptune and Queen Codfish and all necessary baby gear were loaded aboard.

Both parents (and the five crew) were apprehensive, though it was not until they were well into the trip that they admitted as much. *Lion* was a racing boat, not fitted out with cabins for comfortable cruising. The galley was minimal. Wet sails and wet-weather gear hung about everywhere. Heading into the Pacific for the first three stormy weeks, when Pippa had to keep Sarah-Jane below, were described by Pippa as unbelievably difficult. Once a day Sarah-Jane would be handed in a safety harness up to her father on deck, for a breath of fresh air.

Overall it was a memorable, fun trip for the family and the very accommodating crew, with stops at Easter Island and the Galapagos Islands, the Panama Canal, two ports in the Caribbean and Ireland. One bonus was that young Miss Blake arrived in England fully potty-trained!

The warm-up races in England reinforced Peter's concerns about

Two-year-old Sarah-Jane Blake crosses the Equator with King Neptune and Queen Codfish.

Baby in a Bucket! Aboard Lion New Zealand *coasting along in the tropics.*

Lion. The inescapable fact was that he had asked for a boat of 31 tons actual weight and *Lion* weighed in at close to 38 tons: some 20% heavier than what he wanted. All he had to offset the weight was a strong boat that in the worst seas, wouldn't break apart.

Only on the way to the start area off Portsmouth did he share some troubling thoughts with his 22 crew. She was, he told them, the strongest boat in the race with the best crew, and she would be there at the finish as some of her competitors might not be. But she was heavier and shorter than the Bruce Farr maxis like *UBS Switzerland*, and there might be times when she would need all the help she could get, if she was to keep up. All he could ask was for everyone's best shot; after that, nature would take its course.

The race was started a month later to catch better weather in the Southern Ocean. However, the conditions on the first leg nearing Cape Town fully tested the leading maxis, with one dismasted and two others significantly damaged. *Lion* had torn her mainsail but otherwise came through with flying colours, second to *UBS Switzerland*. Perhaps they'd got her right after all.

In the Southern Ocean, their hope proved false. From Cape Town to Auckland and on to Cape Horn, the southern winds were 'too light, too fickle,' according to one skipper. Peter felt cheated. He wrote that the later start, 'had changed the character of the race … if we hadn't sighted icebergs and seen Cape Horn in daylight, it would have been difficult to believe that we had been in the Southern Ocean at all.'

Lion arrived a distant fifth in Auckland — though still enjoying a stunning Waitemata reception from the crowds on the water and spectators round the harbour. She was second in Punta del Este in Uruguay, and third across the line in Portsmouth. Overall, behind *UBS Switzerland*, she was second fastest around the world. Peter wrote in his log that it was:

> *No mean effort ... I have no doubt that I had the best crew in the race. I am only sad that the boat we sailed wasn't quite as highly capable ... But* Lion *was the boat we had and* Lion *was the boat we would sail to the maximum. We pushed her as hard as possible to see if the rest could sustain the same sort of pressure. The outcome might have been different had the conditions been more Whitbread-normal, but they weren't — and that, as they say is yacht racing.* (Sir Peter Blake, An Amazing Life, p. 166)

Another Whitbread, another profound disappointment. They'd had no major breakages or disasters. *Lion*'s three encounters with whales and a few sunfish, which were not inconsiderable because at 1000 kg sunfish are the world's heaviest bony fish, had only been minor bumps.

Peter and crew on Lion New Zealand *on a late-night arrival during the fourth Whitbread race.*

In some ways, Peter said, she was the right boat for the wrong race. Or perhaps, the wrong race for the right boat. But the young crew had given it their best shot and in all their port visits they had been 'tremendous ambassadors for New Zealand.' One crew member said, 'we went back to sea for a rest.'

For many of the 22 crew, the *Lion* campaign kick-started their careers as top-class, well-paid professional yachtsmen, moving directly from *Lion* to *Steinlager 2* and the New Zealand America's Cup campaigns.

'With *Ceramco* and then *Lion*,' says Grant Dalton, 'Peter created a family of yachtsmen who became the heart of New Zealand sailing ... There was nothing obvious that Peter did to hold it all together. But it was a magical mix and an absolute credit to him. We were all quite young, all on an adventure, and he was the glue that made it all work.'

Because of the experience on *Lion*, Peter had grown as a leader. For *Ceramco* he was the initiator, the skipper, fundraiser, shore manager, and increasingly, publicist. For the bigger, more complex *Lion* campaign, while still the skipper and in effect the CEO, he found that much more responsibility had to be entrusted to his team members. Developing delegation and leadership skills that only succeeded through using good communication was a solid grounding for the even bigger campaigns that were to come. In both New Zealand campaigns, Peter quickly learned the value of keeping his sponsors, the media and the public in touch with what was happening, at all hours of the day and night and from the middle of the ocean. Today it's called 'branding', but to Peter it was just keeping faith

A weary skipper.

with the people who'd shown their faith in him and his crew.

Peter would always say that, despite everything, he had fond memories of the Lion campaign. Of all his Whitbread attempts, it had been the source of the most fun.

However, the record book shows that despite finishing the whole circumnavigation second fastest, Lion New Zealand, aka 'The Urban Assault Vehicle', finished seventh on handicap.

Choosing a course

Crossing the oceans in a square-rigger carrying cargo or passengers, or on a racing yacht under sail, the best and quickest course would be the shortest — right? The navigator would simply plot the shortest course towards where you wanted to go.

Not necessarily. Not even mostly. Skippers of vessels under sail learned many centuries ago that some of the winds that whistle around our planet are stronger than others, or blow from more useful directions.

Some, like the Southern Ocean's Roaring Forties, blow hard and continuously. Others, like the areas near the equator known as the Doldrums, can have flat oily calms for weeks on end.

There are also the ocean's currents and tides to take into account. Currents move as continuous flows of water, generated mostly by wind, the earth's rotation and temperature. Either as wind-driven surface currents or deeper ocean currents, they flow for long distances, and greatly influence our climate. The Gulf Stream, which cools northwestern Europe, the California current around Hawaii, and the Labrador current, are well-known examples of ocean currents.

Skippers must also consider coastal tides; that is, the rise and fall of sea levels caused by the pull of the moon and sun. Coastal dwellers will be familiar with the tides predictably coming in and going out, usually two high and two low each 24-hour period.

From the 15th century and through the great ages of sail and exploration, ships' masters and mapmakers began to build huge banks of knowledge about our planet's winds, ocean currents and tides. It was important for the trading ships to carry their often-perishable cargoes from India and Asia back to Europe in the shortest possible time. Ships carrying migrants naturally wanted the quickest possible routes.

Until powered ships took over in the late 19th century, tall ships' masters used their knowledge of the favourable winds, such as the Trades, or the prevailing westerlies of the northern hemisphere. The clipper route through the southern Atlantic and into the Southern Ocean was especially important, with the Roaring Forties blowing thousands of immigrant and cargo ships towards the Far East, Australia and New Zealand.

Today's merchant and passenger ships with their powerful engines can mostly choose the shortest routes. However, their navigators still take weather patterns and forecasts very much into account, using the sophisticated satellite and computer technology now available.

Maxi ocean racers also use GPS technology to plot their best courses. The boats may sail many hundreds of miles apart, completely out of sight of one another, or they might stay in close company, as in match racing. Good race navigators are prized for their ability to pick favourable weather systems. But instinct, experience, judgement and luck also come into play. The successful skipper in long-distance ocean racing is the one who gets it right more often than others.

6

Around Australia on *Steinlager 1*

On New Year's Eve 1986, James Blake arrived in the world. His mother, in labour and hearing from her hospital room the clink of glasses and the nurses 'yahooing up' as midnight approached, hoped he might delay his entrance until January 1. That was his grandfather's birthday. But James had other ideas. He arrived two hours before the clocks struck 12. Quite typical, his mum would say. This was a baby that would start walking at 11 months!

Peter was home in Emsworth that snowy winter, enjoying a brief interlude of normality with his family and especially the new baby. He was an enthusiastic, hands-on father who 'probably changed as many nappies as I did', says Pippa. Between nappies and taking Sarah-Jane for sled rides in the snow, however, Peter was doing some hard thinking about his next career move.

Few people besides Pippa knew that his plans involved rather more than just a fifth and hopefully successful Whitbread. He had slogged around the world four times in a monohull and, for pressing reasons of 'unfinished business', would do so again. That was a given. Pippa knew that his pronouncements after each long race, which included 'it was too tough', 'he'd never do it again', 'he was stopping, settling down, they'd buy a farm, go inland!', would be quietly forgotten as Peter contemplated a new sailing challenge.

Perhaps thinking back to the Round Britain event in 1974

where even smallish multihulls had outclassed longer monohulls, Peter was now keen to test himself in a large and very fast multihull. In his mind was a different sort of race around the world: non-stop in a fast, probably multihulled yacht that was not restricted in any way by ratings or design rules. Just the fastest boat and the most daring crew. There was also the interesting prospect of a Two-man Round Australia Race being run in 1988 as part of Australia's bicentennial celebrations. So, he needed three boats, two of them multihulls. All would be state-of-the-art design, employing the best New Zealand boat-builders and sail-makers he could find, and the best crew. It was a bold, audacious package, even by Peter's standards.

Lion Breweries' head Douglas Myers had been a great sponsor of the *Lion* campaign; perhaps that was where he should start. The story is told that early in 1988 Peter met Douglas Myers to discuss what the future might hold. Lion Breweries, unaware of *Lion*'s weight problems, had been more than satisfied with its sponsorship of the *Lion* campaign. Especially noted had been Peter's willingness to 'bend over backwards' to be very supportive, even protective, of his sponsor. Now, Myers readily agreed to sponsor Peter's proposal for an 'around-the-world-in-80-days' boat, either a trimaran or a big catamaran. Peter recalled,

Peter was now keen to test himself in a large and very fast multihull.

> *I was walking out the door and I said: 'I don't suppose you're interested in the Whitbread any more?' And he said: 'Oh, with* Lion New Zealand *that was too good for us. Promotionally we can't let that go.' So I went and sat down again and then we had a Whitbread as well. We had a look at the whole thing and came up with boat number three, which was a trimaran (which*

> *would be* Steinlager 1*). We then reversed everything and decided we'd do the trimaran thing first followed by the Whitbread and then have a think about the third one, depending on how the company was going, the profile and everything else. (Richard Becht,* Sir Peter Blake: A Pictorial Salute, *p. 19)*

So the 'Steinlager Challenge' was born: three boats, $6 million worth. For Lion Breweries, who were looking to expand their operations and profile in Australia and beyond, it would be promotional money well spent. In corporate circles, where sponsorship was fast becoming big business, yachting and rugby were considered the best 'vehicles' for taking New Zealand's name and potential to the world. The key was Peter himself, his many achievements, his huge public profile, his managerial style and proven leadership.

As Douglas Myers later said, 'When he came to me with this idea of three events — that's when I probably started to view him as an adventurer on a world basis, and not just a yachtie. It all sounded good stuff, but it was more just supporting him really …'

For Peter and Pippa, these new and ambitious plans heralded major changes in their lives. The Steinlager Challenge would involve more money and many more people, including public relations consultants, people to organise food and other jobs which up until now Peter, with Pippa and his loyal team, had largely done themselves. For the first time in his life Peter and his colleagues were on a proper salary.

Pippa was finding that organising and travelling with two children were somewhat harder than with one child. She was determined that she and the children would remain part of Peter's life no matter how many boats he was planning, building or racing.

Given the green light from his sponsor, Peter began looking for designers and crew, initially for the Two-man Round Australia

Steinlager 1, *Peter's first multi-hull built for the Two-man Round Australia race, 'flying a hull.'*

event in *Steinlager 1*. Not too far behind, preliminary planning of *Steinlager 2* for the 1989–90 Whitbread race also began. There wasn't a great deal of time for either, let alone both and happening more or less at the same time.

Steinlager 1 was 'exhaustingly fast,' a futuristic monster trimaran. She was 60 feet (18 metres) long and 52 feet (15.8 metres) across — that's wider than a tennis court and, in fact, not far off square! She had an unusual wing mast, wider and thinner than a conventional mast. Built of carbon fibre and Kevlar cloth impregnated with resin, she would be exceptionally strong, light and speedy.

New Zealand, and even Australia, had never seen anything like it, and many older Kiwi yachties, suspicious of multihulls, looked on in disbelief. Her designer was David Alan-Williams, an Englishman whom Peter had met during his time on *Burton Cutter* and *Heath's Condor*. Alan-Williams was experienced and respected for his multihull designs.

Getting the hull from the Auckland boatyard to the water was a mission. No heavy-lift helicopter was available,

> ... so we had to go around measuring road widths. Eventually we got her to a shallow creek in the middle of a stormy night after removing half a dozen power poles, a number of lamp posts and a bus shelter. We even used two cranes to lift her over some tall trees, one passing it to the other and then on to a barge. (Adventurer, p. 54)

Launched by Pippa, who wielded an outsized bottle of the sponsor's fine product, *Steinlager 1* was shipped to Sydney. Peter had already chosen the partner he wanted to race with: 31-year-old Mike Quilter, one of his *Lion* team-mates, who'd gone straight from *Lion* to join the America's Cup team in Fremantle, Western Australia. Blakey just happened to call by in Fremantle, Mike recalls, and 'once you'd sailed with Peter — I don't know what it was — you'd always go around with him again. You'd never say no. He'd say, "Come on," and you would say, "Yep, I'm off, I'm with you."'

That Fremantle visit wasn't just about the Round Australia race. Peter was also determined to recruit the best possible crew for *Steinlager 2*. By the time he left, a small band of top Kiwi sailors had committed to him for the campaign.

Mike Quilter, known internationally as 'Lowlife' or 'Lowie', became Peter's most trusted man on a boat. With considerable experience of classic offshore races in England, Hawaii and Australia, Mike had applied to join *Lion* because 'you couldn't shut the *Ceramco* boys up ... ' At parties Mike heard them tell *Ceramco* jokes and *Ceramco* stories, they never stopped talking about *Ceramco*. 'I decided that anything that had that much effect on their lives must be a good thing to do.'

Their 7000-mile (11,265 kilometre) race around the world's biggest island started in Sydney on 8 August, and they ran

> Steinlager 1 *was 'exhaustingly fast'*

straight into trouble. Out of the Sydney Heads into the Pacific, they were hit by a 55-knot southerly gale whipping up huge seas. Twice, while her crew held their breath, the monster trimaran threatened to flip over. Peter reported,

> We weren't all that sure what she could take and, while getting sail down, we landed sideways on top of a big sea with both starboard float and the main hull out of the water at an angle of about 30 degrees. For the moment we hung there not knowing if she would capsize or flop back into the water again ... ' (Adventurer, p. 58)

That night, for the first time in his life, Mike Quilter chundered from nerves: not from fear, but 'nervous that we might flip the boat, or drop the rig and not win the race, nervous that we might stuff up this beautiful boat on the first night at sea ... but Peter was such a big rooster, so calm and so strong.'

Pippa, back home with the children, was feeling the strain, only too aware of the dangers of fast multihull sailing. In extreme conditions, which *Steinlager 1* was bound to face, trimarans had been known to flip on to their sides, or break apart. Many years later, she wrote that 'for the first time, I was worried about Peter at sea.' She and the children made many long flights to ensure that even if the boat arrived at a stopover in the middle of the night, they would be on the dock to welcome him.

Even before the first stops in Queensland, it was clear that *Steinlager 1* was streets ahead of the opposition, on occasion reaching a staggering 33 knots. You can water-ski behind a boat going that fast! Peter described it as 'adrenalin-pumping, knife-edged sailing at its best.' The unconventional wing-mast proved its worth, keeping the 'Flying Stein' going comfortably by itself through storms and squalls too strong to carry any sail.

Below, in the sparsely-fitted main cabin, it was no picnic. A trimaran's motion is quite different from a monohull, and except in flat calms, can be jerky and unpredictable. In big seas the movement is violent.

A make-shift bunk was rigged up directly under the cockpit so that a line from the helmsman on deck could be tied to the sleeping crew's big toe. A yank on the line meant 'Help!'

Around the top of Australia to Darwin, down to Fremantle, east to Adelaide, Hobart and Southport (Victoria), *Steinlager 1* found her true opposition was whatever the elements could throw at her. They had calms and suffocating tropical heat off the Northern Territories and 60 knots for days on end across the notorious Great Australian Bight.

Steinlager 1 was the only boat to come through the race unscathed and undamaged. At least one trimaran was flipped, two monohulls were lost, and tragically, on that stormy first night, one crewman was lost overboard. At each of the seven stops Peter and Mike were greeted by the travelling roadshow comprising shore-support staff in two 4-wheel drive vehicles. The vehicles carried more than 30 pieces of luggage, including merchandise for selling at each port. Pippa and the children and other sailing wives usually flew in, sometimes braving 'remarkably small planes.'

A special birthday needed to be celebrated in Hobart: Peter's 40th. Knowing that Peter could play the ukulele, probably from his *Bandit* and *Ladybird* days, Pippa 'scoured Hobart' to buy him one. He was too exhausted to play it though, ending his 40th party with his head on the restaurant table, fast asleep.

They still had to get their monster boat across the dangerous Bass Strait to the last stopover in Southport before the gruelling race ended.

There was one reward to be savoured with the family before Peter returned to his full-on role of chief executive for the *Steinlager 2* campaign. With three crew, the Blake family took a short holiday on *Steinlager 1*. The cabin below provided only two bunks, so it was a bit like a floating camping holiday. With the trimaran barrelling along 40-knot winds, Pippa would describe the experience of being stuck below for two hours, harnessed to her children, like to being in a washing machine.

Up on deck, Peter was, no doubt, in his element.

Why are trimarans the fastest of all sailing boats?

Multihulls, or proa, are the swiftest boats under sail. They date back 4000 years to fast, light craft developed by Polynesians in the Pacific Islands, used for fishing and to travel between islands.

A trimaran has three components: a main or centre hull (known to the Polynesians as the vaka) and two outrigger hulls, called floats or amas. The main hull and floats are connected by 'wings'. Cruising or regular trimarans have solid wings that incorporate the cabin. On open or racing trimarans the wings are weight-reducing open sheets of netting, and accommodation is only in the main hull. Compared with a monohull of the same length, a trimaran will be considerably faster. This is because it can raise more sail, can sail in shallower water and, with less wetted area, is faster. In strong winds it can remain more upright than a monohull.

Because they are so wide, trimarans do not have the heavy lead keels that keep monohulls from capsizing and they can sail a straighter line. But tacking and gybing can be tricky, and there is less living space inside their narrower hulls.

Sailed carefully, adjusting sails to the speed and conditions, trimarans are safe craft. Flipping or capsizing sideways is unusual, but in high winds and steep seas a tri can sometimes flip end-over-end, or pitchpole. Sometimes, in extreme conditions, skippers put out sea anchors and trail lines simply to slow a trimaran down.

A capsized trimaran is usually unsinkable because the upper hull is enough to keep the boat afloat. But they are harder to turn upright than monohulls. Sideways pulling can damage the mast and rigging; sometimes they are successfully righted end-over-end. Another safety advantage is that their speed means skippers can swiftly return to port or seek shelter in deteriorating conditions.

During the 1950s, multihulls grew in popularity. Early enthusiasts in the United States were Victor Tchetchet, a Russian émigré artist living in New York who built two plywood 24-foot trimarans, *Eggnog 1* and *Eggnog 2*; and Arthur Piver, who also designed trimarans popular with amateur boatbuilders. Victor Tchetchet probably coined the word 'trimaran'.

In 2008, French sailor Francis Joyon set a new world record for solo non-stop circumnavigation, his 95-foot (28.9 metre) *Trimaran IDEC* taking 57 days, 13 hours, 34 minutes, 6 seconds. He beat the record held by British sailor Ellen MacArthur, set February 2005, of just over 71 days at sea.

The Trophée Jules Verne for the fastest non-stop crewed circumnavigation has been held by both trimarans and catamarans. Since Bruno Peyron of France set the first record of 79 days, 22 hours, 17 minutes and 22 seconds in 1993, the record has steadily dropped because of ever bigger, lighter but stronger boats. The current holder is Loïck Peyron, younger brother of Bruno, whose 130-foot (28.9 metre) trimaran *Banque Populaire V* went round the world in 45 days, 13 hours, 42 minutes and 53 seconds.

In recent years the trimaran concept has been employed for warships, and car ferries capable of carrying up to 350 cars. Trimarans are now popular for recreational boating, especially in America, designed with floats that fold up to allow the boat to be taken on a trailer.

In 2010 the America's Cup was raced for the first time in multihulls, the American trimaran *BMW Oracle* beating the Swiss catamaran *Alinghi*. The 2013 regatta in San Francisco is the first to be raced in 72-foot (21.9 metre) wing-sail catamarans.

7

Whitbread glory on *Steinlager 2*

The start of a great ocean yacht race is a fantastic spectacle. After the jockeying for position before the final gun, there they go — seemingly so serene, so controlled. As the boats gather speed, they leave feathery trails of wash. Eager powerboats are kept at bay so they don't disturb the water surface or worse, cause a furious skipper to change course. Usually, the bigger boats start moving to the front of the fleet.

Although in 'race mode', skippers and crew are usually giving a huge sigh of relief. Now, finally, they are being left alone to do what they do best: making a boat go as fast as possible. All the anguish over hull designs, rigs, sails, provisions, all the talking, the press conferences, the gamesmanship, the allegations of cheating, all the gym sessions, being nice to sponsors and little old ladies who donated $20 — it's all left behind.

Each boat is its own small world. The crew settle into watches. The cook is busy in the galley, the navigator at his computers plotting the best course. They carry only what provisions, fuel, medical and other supplies are deemed necessary through expert calculation. They have thousands of miles to go. Sea fever is calling.

Plain sailing? The path of *Steinlager 2* towards the majestic Whitbread race start off Southampton on 2 September 1989 had been anything but.

To begin, the rules had changed. Previous races had gone to ports around the old clipper ship route: England to Cape Town, to Auckland, round the Horn to somewhere on the eastern coast of South America, then back to Portsmouth. Three stops.

Now, avoiding Cape Town because of South Africa's political troubles, and increasing the stopovers to six, the organisers had decided on a completely new circuit. The race would go from Southampton to Punta del Este in Uruguay, across the southern Atlantic to Fremantle then to Auckland, then round Cape Horn and back to Punta del Este, up to Fort Lauderdale on America's eastern seaboard and finally back across the northern Atlantic to Southampton.

The course meant more downwind sailing than ever.

Before they left to do the Round Australia race, Peter and Mike Quilter had travelled to Annapolis to talk to designer Bruce Farr. They wanted the longest boat they could afford, and out of the blue Peter asked, could it possibly be a ketch?

That was a pretty far-out suggestion. There had been no successful two-masted maxis in the racing scene for some 20 years. What they did not know at the time was that Grant Dalton had overhead the word 'ketch' at a barbecue in Annapolis and, thinking something was up, had asked Bruce Farr the same question! Bruce ran the concept through his computer. Yep, a masthead ketch looked pretty good. But Peter was thinking of his beloved family ketch, *Ladybird*, with her easily managed fractional rig, meaning smaller headsails and a larger mainsail.

Farr wasn't enthusiastic, but after two hours' hard talking he ran a fractional ketch through the computer. On the screen the boat got longer, and the masts higher. 'A rocket ship emerged,' recalls Quilter.

Peter's new, and last, challenger for the Whitbread would be huge: 85 feet (25.9 metres) long, with a huge main and huge mizzen. Peter and Mike left Farr's office elated, with the basic drawing of 'something really special' in their briefcases.

> ## What is a fractional rig?
>
> On a yacht a fractional rig is easily identifiable when a foresail (jib or genoa) doesn't reach all the way to the top of the mast. The foresail is rigged on a wire stay running from the bow to a point about two-thirds the way up.
>
> The advantages of fractional rig are that the mast can be set further forward, allowing for a larger mainsail and smaller foresails. A yacht with fractional rig is easier to sail and typically used for dinghies and medium-sized racing keelers. Throughout the 20th century most small yachts have been designed with fractional rigs.
>
> With recent improvements in sail cloth, designers have moved to the simpler masthead rig, where the forestay goes to the top (or nearly the top) of the mast. This rig is more traditional and common for larger keelers or cruising yachts. Masthead yachts are easier to tune and, some think, more secure. They can carry bigger spinnakers on downhill runs.
>
> Both types of rig have their supporters who are passionate about the advantages of the one over the other.

She wouldn't be a comfortable boat. To keep her as light as possible, she'd have only the basics: dry bunks and an efficient galley that could produce hot food under any conditions. To save weight there would be no heater for the Southern Ocean, a decision later regretted. She'd have fewer hatches than usual to keep out even the worst seas crashing across the deck. And she'd have this weird, very unfashionable fractional rig.

The team in Auckland, initially dubious about a fractional-rigged ketch, began to get as excited as their boss. Peter and Mike left to do the Round Australia race. This wasn't as crazy as it might have seemed. The *Steinlager 2* project was well under way and Peter implicitly trusted the people he'd put in charge. Besides, it would turn out that the navigation and other electronic systems tested on *Steinlager 1* would be valuably applied to *Steinlager 2*.

All was going according to plan for the Steinlager Challenge.

Three days before the Round Australia start, Peter faced

Steinlager 2, *in the Solent, heading for victory in the 1989 Fastnet race.*

a catastrophe. In a phone call from Auckland he was told that *Steinlager 2*'s carbon fibre hull had a major construction problem and would have to be scrapped.

He rushed back to Auckland to talk to Douglas Myers and Lion Nathan's bosses. They didn't hesitate. Start again! It would cost an extra $1 million but they had time, and it had to be done. Their confidence in Peter and the project was complete. Peter recalled that everyone was 'convinced we were on to a winner.'

The old hull was cut up, new moulds were built and 17 weeks later a new shiny red hull, complete with deck, stood proudly in the Auckland shed. It was agreed that the lessons learned from this expensive and nearly disastrous setback had given them a better hull.

As the carefully guarded secrets about the two Kiwi ketches came out, the rivalry between Peter Blake and his former *Lion* watch captain, Grant Dalton, heated up.

The yachting community was agog. *Steinlager 2* was to be a fractional rig. Everyone knew this was Peter's last crack at the Whitbread prize. Many of Peter's crew had sailed with him before and knew about his relaxed leadership style. But Grant Dalton had scored major sponsorship from whiteware manufacturer Fisher & Paykel and he was also building a ketch! It too, was a Farr design, a little smaller but with a masthead rig. Dalton's crew of tough, strong men, similar to himself, would push *Fisher & Paykel* hard, harder, he made it known, than Blake pushed his own craft. Dalton was 26, had done two Whitbreads and was hungry for personal success on his third.

Before being shipped to England, trial races between the maxis were agreed. Neither boat seemed to have the advantage, although *Fisher & Paykel* beat *Steinlager 2* in a classic Auckland event around the Hauraki Gulf.

The notorious Fastnet race from Plymouth to Ireland showed that the Whitbread was likely to be an epic battle between the two Kiwi ketches. It was, said one observer, 'just a bloodbath!' Leaving all the sloop-rigged (single-masted) maxis in their wake, they fought out a fierce private duel. *Fisher & Paykel* led much of the way, but near the finish *Steinlager 2* slipped past to cross the line not quite three minutes ahead.

However, before the Whitbread race began, Peter and Grant Dalton joined forces to fight a different sort of battle. No doubt alarmed at the Kiwi ketches' runaway success in the Fastnet race, several senior British skippers accused the Kiwis of cheating. While in New Zealand, both ketches had been carefully measured six times to ensure that they complied with the strict design rules. Now, in Southampton, after some very minor modifications, they were measured again and cleared for the start.

The unpleasant mind games didn't stop there. On the eve of the start, the skippers attended a press conference. Peter was the only one who had done all four Whitbreads, and after so dramatically winning the Fastnet, he was considered a favourite. But one of the British skippers involved in the measurement accusations used the occasion to attack Peter personally. In his opinion, he told the gathering, Blake was an experienced seaman and a good navigator, but simply not a winner. He'd never come close to winning a Whitbread, had never won any yacht race of significance (apparently the Fastnet, Sydney to Hobart and Round Australia races didn't count) and he would not win this Whitbread. Peter Blake was a loser. It was that simple.

According to *Steinlager* crew Mark Orams, who was present, Peter showed great restraint, calmly replying that we would have to wait and see if the British skipper was right. But his crew knew that inside he was steaming. They were steaming. Now they had extra motivation to show what *Steinlager 2* could do.

On 2 September 1989 the Whitbread fleet of 21 sloops and two ketches assembled for the start off Southampton. Originating from 13 nations, it was the strongest fleet so far.

Off the coast of Portugal Peter made a decision that won them the first 6281-mile (10,108 kilometre) leg and ultimately, the race. They would head out into the Atlantic to catch more favourable winds. Some on board, including Mike Quilter, were dubious, but Peter stuck to his guns. It was the right call, based as much on instinct and courage as navigational skill. *Steinlager* clocked up a Whitbread record, a whopping 343 miles (552 kilometres) in one day, averaging 14.3 knots, and was soon 80 miles (128 kilometres) ahead of the next boat and 270 miles (434 kilometres) ahead of *Fisher &Paykel*.

No long-distance race is ever plain sailing. Sitting in the Doldrums for a day or so had reduced *Steinlager*'s lead. Her satnav equipment temporarily failed, causing Peter to

Father and son James reunited in Brest (Brittany) at the finish of the successful non-stop circumnavigation in the catamaran ENZA New Zealand, *April 1994.*

dig out his sextant and happily navigate the old-fashioned way for two days. With 600 miles (965 kilometres) to go, the 35-knot wind came frustratingly dead ahead. Peter made another good call, to sail conservatively, avoiding damage, towards Punta del Este. Others behind were not so lucky, or so wise. *Fisher & Paykel* lost her mizzen mast. The British skipper who'd insulted Peter at the press conference had his boat fall heavily off a wave, cracking the deck.

For Peter, it was a spectacular start to his campaign. *Steinlager 2* arrived in Punta del Este 11 hours ahead of the next to finish, with *Fisher & Paykel* 32 hours behind.

The margin was too great for the skipper who had publicly called Peter a loser. (The same skipper later claimed he was just winding up the opposition!) The skipper flew back to England during the stop-over to demand that all the yachts be remeasured.

Peter couldn't let the insinuations of cheating pass. He'd insisted from the beginning that *Steinlager 2*, and the way she was sailed, complied with the rules. He reminded race officials of the measuring that had been done, the checks and double-checks of hull, sails and rigging, both in Auckland and Southampton.

'I don't know what more we can do,' he told one reporter. 'You don't win this kind of race by fiddling with the yacht's rating. You win with good tactics and a well-fed and motivated crew.' The race officials agreed, and the affair blew over. It made Peter and his crew more determined to leave the British skipper's maxi well in their wake.

For the next leg, 7650 miles (12,311 kilometres) from Uruguay across the bottom of the world to Fremantle, this outcome was theoretically unlikely. *Steinlager 2* was the heaviest boat in the fleet, and in the Southern Ocean the other maxis, including *Fisher & Paykel*, should be faster. For much of the leg *Steinlager 2* trailed behind at least three others. Making the decision to go further south, risking icebergs, *Steinlager 2* began to haul in the leaders. The unrelenting gales and sub-Antarctic latitude were taking their toll on boat and crew. Rigging was damaged, the decks were slippery with snow and ice and the conditions in the unheated cabin were not pleasant.

After three weeks of hell, they turned north. Finding the lighter airs that suited her, *Steinlager 2* passed all her rivals and headed into the final approaches to Fremantle. She was an hour-and-a-half ahead of the next maxis, and three hours clear of *Fisher & Paykel*.

First across the line and handicap honours, again! Another double-whammy! If Peter was starting to dream of holding the Whitbread Trophy aloft, he also knew there was a long way to go yet.

The third and shorter leg, from Fremantle to Auckland, has been recorded as one of the greatest duels in the history of long-distance racing. Virtually from the firing of the gun, Peter Blake and Grant Dalton eyed each other across dangerously narrow and rough stretches of water. Several times in the huge seas one or other maxi had to take avoiding action to prevent a collision.

It was brutal match-racing in the middle of the ocean. If the Fastnet had been 'a bloodbath,' that was just a warm-up. By the time the two ketches approached Cape Reinga, New Zealand's northwesterly tip, word of the duel was out. To the crews' astonishment, hundreds of spectators were watching from the clifftops, along with a flotilla of fishermen in the water. Television crews were in action. Their epic battle had become prime-time news.

What happened next has passed into legend. Rounding North Cape and turning south to Auckland, only 200 miles (321 kilometres) away, Peter decreed that all hands would stay on deck until the finish. Throughout the night, passing the Bay of Islands and then Whangarei Heads, they grimly defended their lead. Peter was about a mile ahead, a useful margin, but running downwind where the trailing boat often picks up a freshening breeze before the leading yacht. After 3000 miles (4828 kilometres) of racing, the gap between the two seemed to be closing.

Off Kawau Island, thinking the sky over Auckland looked a bit ominous, Mike Quilter went below to listen to weather reports. On Newstalk ZB he heard a Titirangi listener say that a 30-knot southerly front had just passed through. As a long-time Auckland yachtie, Peter knew what this meant. Already he could see the southerly change churning up the surface of the water ahead. They needed to drop the downwind sails, spinnaker and mizzen staysail, and fast. 'Get rid of it!' he yelled from the helm.

When the southerly hit *Steinlager*, the spinnaker had been skilfully dropped and she was ready. Dalton had watched his rival's spinnaker disappear with some bemusement, but when the southerly very soon hit *Fisher & Paykel* he realised why. Too late! His crew eventually got the spinnaker down, but by the time they'd sorted out the mess and the new upwind sails were drawing, *Steinlager* was again a mile (1.6 kilometres) clear.

With about 16 miles (25.7 kilometres) to go, the match-race was effectively over. At the wheel, Peter was heard to murmur, 'Got the bastards!' Even so, at the finish, there was only six minutes in it.

Auckland turned on a mighty and emotional welcome, for both the valiant Kiwi ketches and later, for the British, European and American maxis and the rest of the fleet that followed them in. Thousands of boats thronged the Waitemata and cheering spectators lined the waterfront roads and high vantage points.

Pippa and the children were dockside. It was always sensational to be there for each arrival, she would later say. The presence of the family helped to rejuvenate Peter for the next leg.

Three down, three double-whammies. Three to go! Could they do it? Peter anticipated that he'd be pushed every inch of the way, principally by *Fisher & Paykel* but also the leading sloops.

Leaving a huge Waitemata Harbour farewell, by the tenth day and deep in the Southern Ocean, the two Kiwi ketches were again match-racing, even as they kept a wary eye not only on each other, but all around for icebergs. Sometimes the speedo was reading 25 knots, and at the bottom of the troughs between monster breaking waves, the boat was completely submerged in white water.

'But *Steinlager 2* always pulled her head up and we often looked at each other with crazed grins. Mad mariners picnic,' Peter recalled.

Rounding Cape Horn the crew kept their promise to a family back in Auckland and scattered the ashes of an old Cape Horner. *Fisher & Paykel* was only four miles behind and, after an exhilarating but scary run in unpredicted 55-knot winds, this was the order in which they finished at Punta del Este.

Four down, four double-whammies. Two to go.

The fifth leg, nearly 5400 miles (8690 kilometres) up to and beyond the equator, would happily return the fleet to tropical temperatures, to t-shirts and shorts on deck. The racing was just as hot. Emerging from the Doldrums, the Kiwi ketches were second and third, but once into the northeast trade winds, they slipped into the lead and back into match-racing mode.

Steinlager 2 had the edge. Surfing down steep waves in torrential rain, she sailed into Fort Lauderdale eight miles ahead of her archrival and well ahead of the rest of the opposition.

Five down, five double-whammies. One to go.

There were still 3800 miles (6115 kilometres) of the northern Atlantic to cross. On day four, despite the hull having been repainted, the rigs pulled out, everything thoroughly checked while in Punta de Este, there was one nasty surprise to deal with. In the middle of the night, the crew heard a loud bang. A chainplate had cracked and was about to break, meaning that the mizzen mast was now dangerously unsupported. The helmsman immediately threw *Steinlager* into a crash gybe, a frightening experience when the boom swings uncontrolled through a wide arc from one side to the other — but it was absolutely the right thing to do. Repairs were made and the mizzen mast was secured. It was a close call and valuable ground had been lost.

Peter later wrote that the quick-witted and 'make-do' nature of his crew allowed them to keep going.

As they clocked off the miles, Peter knew he had to strike a balance between sailing hard to keep their slim lead and carefully nursing a boat whose gear was inevitably showing signs of wear and tear. Shackles and deck fittings were being replaced too often. It was no comfort to think that other boats would be similarly troubled. 'Once again,' recalled Peter, 'the two Kiwi boats battled for every yard of sea.'

Off the southwestern tip of England a strange situation developed. The Kiwi ketches were becalmed within three boat-lengths of each other. They were close enough to hurl good-natured abuse at each other. It was *Steinlager 2* that first caught the freshening breeze and soon, with all her reaching sails set, she was out-gunning *Fisher & Paykel*. She was nearly home! In Peter's words:

> *A huge spectator fleet whistling and hooting and creating a massive wake, accompanied us up the Solent and then to the finish line near Ocean Village Marina in Southampton.*
>
> *All of a sudden it seemed half of New Zealand were to be found on the quayside. There were literally thousands of people. Some, we were told later, had been waiting there for three days. Then came the crackle of fireworks but they couldn't drown out the noise of cheering and shouting.*
>
> *It was time at last to claim the Whitbread Trophy. After four unsuccessful attempts the victory this time was particularly sweet.* (Adventurer, p. 76)

Steinlager 2, every stitch of sail set triumphantly aloft, had crossed the line only 36 minutes in front of *Fisher & Paykel*. As their formidable rivals pulled into the marina, the *Steinlager* team spontaneously joined in the crowd's applause. For New Zealand, it had been an epic battle and a double triumph.

With six line honours and six handicap wins, *Steinlager*'s achievement was even more special, unprecedented in the history of the Whitbread race. It was unlikely, wrote Pippa, that anyone in future round-world events would ever match that record.

After four attempts over 17 years, totalling nearly 150,000 miles (241,401 kilometres) of ocean racing, Peter was a happy man. He would later attribute his success to his long experience in picking the weather.

Realising a dream — Peter holds aloft the coveted Whitbread Trophy.

> *The biggest factor in any of these long-distance races is the weather. If you go the wrong way — on the first beat in an America's Cup race or at the start of any leg in a race like the Whitbread — you never recover from it. You really have to spend time thinking about the weather and a lot of that comes only from experience at sea and time on the water. You gradually understand that you don't know too much about it, and, if you reach that conclusion, you're halfway there.* (Sir Peter Blake: A Pictorial Salute, *p. 24*)

Peter's Lion Nathan sponsors were equally happy, with sales figures showing dramatic rises in the US, UK and New Zealand and better distribution deals, all largely attributed to the success

Receiving the Sir Bernard Ferguson Trophy for New Zealand Sailor of the Year from then Governor General Sir Keith Holyoake.

of 'Big Red.' Publicly, after the *Steinlager 2* win, Peter was saying, 'Never again — that's it!'

The rewards were coming thick and fast: massive coverage in the international press, an OBE from the Queen, 1990 New Zealand Sportsman of the Year, and his crew New Zealand Sports Team of the Year. He was judged Communicator of the Race by the Whitbread organisation and Communicator of the Year by the Public Relations Institute of New Zealand. In the prestigious American publication *Yachting Magazine*, he was named Yachtsman of the Year.

Time, perhaps, for resting on a laurel or two. Pippa, who knew him better than anyone, didn't really expect him 'to settle down to normal life. He didn't. He carried on with other things. We always talked about having a normal life, but I never knew what a normal life with Peter was.' She knew there were more adventures lurking at the back of his mind. The Trophée Jules

Verne, perhaps, non-stop around the world in any sort of boat you liked! Round the world in a hot-air balloon! Even then, going up the Amazon and to the Antarctic!

As Mike Quilter put it, 'He was always thinking ten years ahead — it was remarkable just how many of his dream projects that he actually did.'

8

Around the World in 80 Days

The Whitbread Race had dominated Peter's life for 17 years. He'd watched the rules change, the number of legs increase and ever greater emphasis placed on speed for its own sake. Although he had no intention of doing another Whitbread, he was not entirely happy with the way things were going. As a figure revered in international sport and a member of the Whitbread managing committee, he was able to say so.

> *At the start there almost certainly was a strong element of people doing the race simply for the hell of sailing around the world, and I really hope that's still the case. If we lose that, it would be a terrible shame.*
>
> *Some of the adventure has been lost in the name of Formula One and in the name of level racing and everything else. The smaller boats, the characters and the problems, that's what the race was all about at first. It was great fun. We used to get together in the ports of call rather than the way it is now where slanging matches have been going on. It's time to turn off the lights and go home if it keeps on going like this.* (Sir Peter Blake: A Pictorial Salute, p. 25)

What were his options, if the Whitbread was behind him and he wanted another long-distance sailing challenge? He knew he hadn't the temperament for sailing solo; sailing with a team of like-minded seafarers was his great love.

What if the emphasis on speed was to become the whole reason for sailing round the world? To be the fastest in any sort of boat, eliminating rules and grumpy rivals making accusations of cheating? How about doing it in a multi-hull, in 80 days?

If the British yachting world concentrated on the Whitbread race in monohulls, and the Americans on America's Cup racing, also in monohulls, French sailors had made long-distance sailing in giant multihulls peculiarly their own. In France, daring and dedicated long-distance racers like Bruno Peyron and Olivier de Kersauson were household names. So, it was to probable French rivals that, shortly after his fourth Whitbread, Peter issued the challenge: try to beat me around the world in 80 days.

Why 80 days? Phileas Fogg, in Jules Verne's novel *Around the World in Eighty Days*, had done just that on land, by rail and where necessary, by steamboat. Modern adventurers would now do it in streamlined racing machines across the uninterrupted oceans.

The Tour du Monde en 80 Jours was formed, an association consisting of Peter as president alongside Robin Knox-Johnson and nine French men and women. Rules were created. In October 1992, at the Yacht Club de France in Paris, Peter

In between projects and races, Peter enjoyed time at home with his family.

announced his intention of crossing the start line off the island of Ushant, France's northwestern tip, in early 1993. It wasn't a race as such, though Peter would have preferred this. Each boat would race against the clock. The course would be simple: leave the Cape of Good Hope and Cape Horn to port and all of Antarctica to starboard. The safety of each boat and crew was the responsibility of each entrant. The fastest time would win the Trophée Jules Verne, an idea first suggested five years earlier by Yves Le Cornec, a French sailor. The winner would keep the trophy until a better time was achieved.

The romantic notion of the race completely captured Peter's imagination, recalls Pippa. 'It was Peter through and through.' He'd already found a mate of like mind. In London, after a brief conversation with his old friend Robin Knox-Johnson, they agreed to pool their resources to find a sponsor.

One was quickly found. Not Douglas Myers and Lion Nathan, who'd decided not to proceed with the third boat of the Steinlager Challenge. This time, it would be another New Zealand company, the New Zealand Apple and Pear Marketing Board (ENZA), whose interest was in promoting New Zealand fruit sales overseas.

Now all that was needed was a suitable boat. Peter and Knox-Johnston flew to Newport, Rhode Island, from where they would sail an 82-foot (25-metre) Canadian-built catamaran called *Tag Heuer* to England. At the boatyard she was lengthened to 85 feet (25.9 metres), given a new carbon fibre mast and a central housing between the hulls for two bunks and the vital electronic equipment. The housing became known as the 'God Pod'.

Before leaving England, Peter had sent his campaign office the estimates for supplies for 77 days at sea for seven people. The buying, sorting and packaging of the mostly freeze-dried packets was Pippa's job. 'Garguantan quantites' of food were involved, and weight was always a worry, but Pippa put in little surprises: cards, presents, fruitcakes, even a blow-up human-sized penguin, to amuse the crew on their endless days at sea.

There were three entrants in the 1993 Trophée Jules Verne. The acclaimed French skipper Bruno Peyron and a crew of four in *Commodore Explorer*; another Frenchman, Olivier de Kersauson in the 90-foot (27.4 metre) trimaran *Charal*; and co-skippers Blake and Knox-Johnston and a crew of five in *Tag Heuer*, now renamed *ENZA New Zealand*.

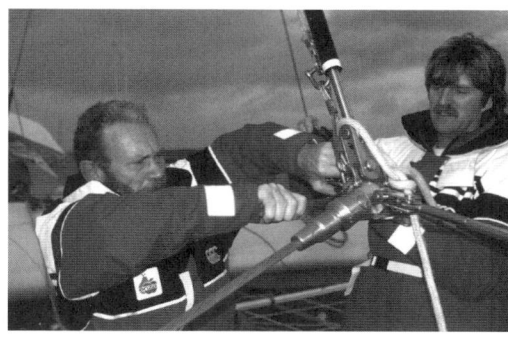

Peter Blake and Robin Knox-Johnston preparing ENZA New Zealand *for their first Trophée Jules Verne attempt, 1992.*

On 28 January 1993, *ENZA* left the French harbour of Brest a few hours before *Commodore* and six days behind *Charal*. By day 17 she was done with the Atlantic and ready to start her long high-speed trundle through the Southern Ocean.

Charal had hit ice and retired to Cape Town. *Commodore* was reportedly going well.

On day 26, 1500 miles (2414 kilometres) to the southeast of Africa's southern tip, Peter recorded, 'Our dream came to a sudden end. In the middle of the night and in one of the world's most inhospitable oceans, we hit an unidentified object, which holed *ENZA*'s starboard hull and she began taking in water fast. We took 16 days to limp back to Cape Town.'

Peter's matter-of-fact summing up of the experience belies what must have been a shattering experience. The unknown object was probably a shipping container floating just beneath the surface, a known hazard for 20th century mariners. Getting back to Cape Town required all his crew's boat-repairing skills, ingenuity and stamina. To keep *ENZA* afloat it was necessary to pump every 15 minutes.

No-one, however, was better equipped to shake off disappointment and say, 'right, let's have another go.' Despite the mishap, *ENZA* was fundamentally sound. The groundwork had

Why catamarans?

A catamaran ('cat' for short) is a two-hulled craft. The design originated in southern India and in the Pacific, where catamarans were built by Polynesians for fishing and voyaging. The word comes from old Tamil, but the modern catamaran is based on Polynesian concepts. It's also probable that two-hulled craft were built in ancient Egypt and Greece.

A famous American designer, Nathanael Herreshoff, built catamarans that demonstrated their speed, but it wasn't until the 1940s that catamarans began to be built seriously by Westerners, initially in Hawaii as racing and ocean-going craft. Small recreational catamarans, designed to be operated from a beach, became popular, especially in America and Australia. Cats perform best in smoother seas, so are specially suitable for recreational coastal cruising. The Tornado class two-person catamaran was an Olympic Games class between 1976 and 2008.

Cats and trimarans are much faster than monohulls. Their hull shape is slimmer and creates less friction in the water; with no keel, they are lighter, more stable and therefore they can carry more sail. They can be tricky to tack, especially if they don't have dagger- or centreboards. In heavy seas, both cats and trimarans are more likely to pitchpole end-over-end rather than capsize sideways.

In recent years the two-hull concept has been favoured for very large, fast, car and passenger ferries. Another type of huge catamaran is the ocean-racing sailboat, some over 100 feet (30 metres) long. Supercats of 150 feet and even over 200 feet in length, designed for corporate and private enjoyment, will soon be seen.

One boost to supercats was the round-world event held in 2000/01 called 'The Race'. Leaving from Barcelona, Spain, with a US$2 million prize, it was the first ever non-stop, no-rules, no-limits, round-the-world sailing contest.

The largest of the seven boats, *PlayStation*, owned by Steve Fossett, was 125 feet (38 metres) long. Most were over 100 feet (30 metres) and capable of speeds up to 50 knots. The Race was won by *Club Med* skippered by Grant Dalton, which took 62 days to circumnavigate the earth at an average of 18 knots.

been done, and the world's imagination, through the international media, had certainly been engaged. Peter once more had unfinished business. Bruno Peyron's *Commodore* had completed her circumnavigation in a record-breaking 79 days, six hours, 15 minutes and 56 seconds. Peyron would hold the Trophée Jules Verne until someone bettered that time.

The decision to make a second attempt was quickly made. Peter told his sponsors that he believed the repaired *ENZA* was absolutely capable of 77 or even 75 days around the world. The sponsors indicated that, despite the mishap, they estimated an achievement of around $100 million worth of media coverage for *ENZA* in European markets. They saw Peter as the perfect ambassador for a quality New Zealand product, and *ENZA* the perfect vehicle.

ENZA was shipped from Cape Town to London and then to Peter's trusted boatbuilders in Auckland. She was substantially modified and strengthened, emerging 93 feet (28.43 metres) long. Her hulls sported a magnificent mural of vividly coloured apples and pears. Visitors inspecting her during a ten-day tour of New Zealand ports were now looking at 'the biggest and probably most seaworthy racing catamaran in the world.'

ENZA's crew would be four Kiwis and four Brits. Six sailors were 'old hands' from *ENZA*'s first attempt. A shore-based router or weatherman, American Bob Rice, would be giving vital daily information and advice on courses from his home in Vermont.

The estimates for the voyage were frightening! They would have to average 15 knots, making better than 350 miles (482 kilometres) a day for 27,500 miles (44,250 kilometres), to arrive in 77 days or less. Peter knew it was a big ask, 'but if the objective was easy, we wouldn't be attempting it.'

Pippa and her crew of helpers swung into action to provision the boat, this time assembling and packing all the food into watertight bins. She began to worry about the coming voyage. 'I was anxious for their safety — probably because of the *Steinlager I* experience.' She knew there were times they would be going at extreme speeds through iceberg country.

This time two giant catamarans would leave Brest together: Peter's *ENZA* and the former *Charal*, now known as *La Lyonnaise des Eaux Dumez*, again with Olivier de Kersauson as skipper. Peter recorded that they 'crossed the Jules Verne start time in a 35-knot northeasterly wind and in very steep seas. Easing the sails and bearing away was a real pleasure and we took off very fast. Six hours later we nearly had to send an "Oops … sorry, New Zealand apple growers" telegram when we missed a huge whale by a few feet.'

They crossed the equator on 23 January, experiencing some of the most incredible sailing imaginable and feeling good about the task ahead.

> *Then came the doldrums. Our speed dropped to 8–10 knots and we were able to get some much needed rest and take advantage of being on deck without foul weather gear. Angus, our youngest recruit, went through his first line-crossing ceremony. I had been doing some gloomy thinking. This had to be my last ocean-racing event as leaving the family yet again had been too hard this time and I was really missing them all. But the weather was now warmer, flying fish had appeared, my bunk was dry and dinner was about to be served.* (Adventurer, p. 88)

On 5 February, now 500 miles (804 kilometres) due south of Cape Town, *ENZA* was visited by a South African Air Force Hercules aircraft. Edited footage of 12 days sailing, plus prepared interviews, were beamed up by microwave link. Peter recorded, 'It was fun chatting with the boys in the Hercules and great to know that the television pictures we were putting out were proving popular worldwide.'

They were 8220 miles into their journey, and well ahead of both *La Lyonnaise* and the record set by *Commodore* the previous year.

Day 24: *ENZA* had been achieving some fantastic daily runs through the Southern Ocean, 440 and more miles a day. On this day, the seas, already mountainous, were still building, and the wind was gusting 55 knots. *ENZA* rose to one particularly steep monster and 'went down the mine' to bury her front third in a wall of water. Peter was just coming up through the hatch, so he couldn't anticipate what happened next and brace himself in time.

> *One moment* ENZA *was doing 28 knots, the next she stopped dead ... I went flying backwards three metres on to the edge of the chart table. There was no obvious boat damage but I was in a lot of pain. 'Doc' Angus, our medic, got his first patient and fed me painkillers for a bruised back and pelvis, and suspected broken ribs.*
>
> *We had to change the watches as I was totally confined to my bunk for several days. From which position I proceeded to give not altogether appreciated sailing instructions to those on deck. My back was so sore that at one point I even considered asking the crew to head directly towards Australia in case I needed to be taken off by helicopter.* (Adventurer, p. 92)

Peter underplayed his injuries. He was in agony, but out of reach of any hospital help for a week. Painkillers, monitoring and meals-on-wheels were all the medic and the crew could provide for him. Peter was 'the spirit of the boat.' If they started together, they finished together. They would — they had to — push on.

His bones slowly mending, Peter used the time in his bunk to catch up with important PR matters like replying to a school near Bordeaux (France) that had written by fax on 8 February expressing great anxiety for *ENZA*'s safety.

'So far it has been extraordinary,' they wrote, 'and for you all we are going to undertake a difficult task to imagine the letters Jules Verne himself would have written to you if he was alive today. Bon courage. Twenty-eight big hearts from the Bordeaux area are beating along with yours.'

Peter replied that it had been 'a bumpy ride,' and gave some domestic details such as the breakfast menu (porridge, scrambled eggs with onion and salami chopped into it, and cups of hot, sweet tea). They had sighted patches of krill that made the water look orange; nearby might be whales, and sure enough, a whale spouted only a short distance away. Then there were the sooty shearwaters, storm petrels and albatrosses flying around the boat, mostly the wandering albatross but also the sooty and black-browed albatross. He wrote that all 'of the crew are fine but looking forward to a few quiet days away from these really confused seas ... we can see Fremantle in Western Australia on the right hand side of the chart ... We are very pleased to know that you are finding this Jules Verne adventure of ours interesting.'

ENZA, with her seriously injured co-skipper, was not merely pushing on, or even keeping her options open for Fremantle.

> *On our 43rd day at sea we were the farthest south a multihull had ever been.*

> *We were advised by [weatherman] Bob Rice that the way was clear for us to head south towards the Antarctic, which we duly did. So for the next 11 days we played dodgems with some of the most beautiful and close-to icebergs I have ever seen.*

> *It was at about this time that the only heater on board, essential for drying cold and wet foul weather gear, gave up on us. Lousy timing. Cooking in the galley was done in full deck gear in order to stay warm and we had to keep a constant 24-hour ice watch with a crew member on the bow.*
>
> *On our 43rd day at sea we were the farthest south a multihull had ever been. 62 degrees south. We received a message from our media team suggesting we pay for extra plotting charts. Theirs only went to 57 degrees south.*
>
> *We kept up our 24 hour watch throughout the time we were in iceberg country with 30 minutes being the longest anyone could take on the bow in the dreadful temperatures. The ice seemed to appear from nowhere, so we constantly had to change direction and wriggle our way through to avoid collision.* (Adventurer, *pp. 96–99*)

By day 47, and with Peter allowed some limited contribution to navigating and helming, *ENZA* was approaching Cape Horn. They were being swept along by monster greybeards, and he was not a happy man.

> *Rounding Cape Horn was a nightmare, as it has been for so many mariners throughout history. Sixty-foot (18 metre) breaking seas and 56-knot northerly winds force us to bare poles (all sails down). I had been around Cape Horn four times before and the conditions this time were the worst I had ever encountered.* ENZA New Zealand *handled them well, but it was knife-edge sailing where we weren't certain if we would see the sun come up the next morning. It was a fantastic learning curve in seamanship.* (Adventurer, *p. 100*)

In other words, even to a sailor who had done seven circumnavigations and sailed more than 400,000 ocean miles (643,737 kilometres), it was a perilous 36 hours hove to, in the very worst the Southern Ocean could hurl at them. Those Cape Horn seas, he said, 'were the ones that would just pick you up and cartwheel you. If one of those broke on top of you, you would just go down and someone else would pick up the pieces afterward.'

Back in the Atlantic, they were deeply grateful to be 'alive, well and still sailing.'

Storming northwards, ENZA was well ahead of the non-stop record, more than five days in fact, and still well ahead of her French rival. But she still had huge icebergs in the vicinity and later, the Doldrums to negotiate. By day 71 she had passed the Azores and was heading for the finish off Ushant, with some 1300 miles (2092 kilometres) to go. They had surely earned a reasonable run home.

The weather gods thought otherwise and threw a last and worst test at ENZA and her exhausted crew. They had been warned a 'really nasty weather front was coming through.' By day 72 winds were gusting up to 55 knots, and ENZA was again down to bare poles,

> ... surfing down huge waves, at a dangerous 20 knots plus. And even worse weather was expected. We had just over 300 miles [482 kilometres] to go.
>
> We were close to losing everything, the record, the boat, and our lives. With winds up to 60 knots, it was all hands on deck as we set to work deploying chains and warps, doubling them up to form a drogue (brake) in a loop from both sterns to keep the catamaran from going end over end. (Adventurer, p. 104)

These 'brakes' were set out 280 feet (85 metres) astern. They slowed *ENZA* down to a controllable 8–10 knots through huge seas and torrential rain.

> *Our final night at sea was as dark and as wild as any we had encountered during the preceding 73 days. With screaming hail squalls and huge cross seas of an estimated 50–60 feet (15–18 metres) we sailed for survival only. The French navy had closed the harbours but having got this far we were coming in regardless …*
> (Adventurer, p. 108)

With less than 200 miles (320 kilometres) to go, *ENZA* was subjected to a full North Atlantic winter storm, but the warps and chains were doing their job, reducing the chance of being pitchpoled or even 'going down the mine' at the eleventh hour.

Soon after dawn on 1 April, Pippa and a film cameraman hovered above *ENZA* aboard the only search-and-rescue helicopter prepared to venture out. To Pippa, *ENZA* looked tiny among the mountainous seas. 'I waved, but they were not looking up. They were concentrating on the job in hand: not to capsize, and to break the record.'

Although she'd spoken to Peter every two or three days throughout the race, Pippa was not aware until the very end of his mishap in the Southern Ocean. Oddly, this had happened very close to where *ENZA* was holed in their first race, forcing her to abandon her first Jules Verne attempt.

Forty-five miles (72 kilometres) from the Ushant finishing line, *ENZA* was joined by a French naval frigate, which escorted her to the finish. Low-flying media helicopters followed her progress. The sirens sounded. *ENZA*, still towing warps and chains from her stern to slow her down, had done it!

Peter later recalled that on board *ENZA*, 'the jubilation was amazing. The total thrill of knowing that not only had we made it around the world and broken the record of all sailing records,

Peter with the sleek Trophée Jules Verne for the fastest non-stop circumnavigation.

but we were home ... We were extremely tired, mentally and physically exhausted, but this took nothing away from the exhilaration of what we had achieved and the pleasure of being back with our families.'

Around the harbour and on the breakwaters, the people of Brest were putting on a huge welcome. This was a seafaring community that understood the sea. 'And we were the non-French boat!' marvelled Peter.

Pippa, Sarah-Jane and James were soon aboard as *ENZA* came alongside the dock. Pippa asked Peter if he was going to do this sort of thing again. His answer was brief: 'No way!' More than 300 international journalists were there to record their reunion.

The stench inside the boat, recalls Pippa, was 'immeasurable.' and Peter's own smell was overpowering. They hadn't changed their clothes for weeks at a time, especially in the Southern Ocean where it was so cold.

Bruno Peyron, the former record holder, was in the crowd to congratulate *ENZA*'s team.

'His eyes clearly said that he had seen what we had seen out there,' Peter wrote of this moment. 'We shared the privileged experience of having sailed around the world in under 80 days. One of our century's last great adventures.'

ENZA's new non-stop global record had easily surpassed Peter's cautious predictions and was officially recorded as 74 days, 22 hours, 17 minutes and 22 seconds. A further 11 world sailing records were set as well, including best 24-hour run under sail, a stunning 520.9 miles (838.3 kilometres) recorded while heading south down the Atlantic.

At a spectacular official ceremony held at the Maritime Museum in Paris, the *ENZA* crew fronted to receive their prize. Sporting smart reefer jackets, team bow ties and red (port) and green (starboard) gloves, they held the Trophée Jules Verne, a sculpture of a slim hull floating on a magnetic field, placed on an aluminum base where previous winners' names are engraved.

A year later Peter was questioned by a journalist about that last so-nearly disastrous day of *ENZA*'s 74-day journey. 'What do you still remember now about what you described as the worst 24 hours of your life?'

'Every second,' he said.

9

'The America's Cup is now New Zealand's Cup!'

As Peter lay injured and frustrated for over a week while sailing through the Southern Ocean, and again during the final 24 hours of the *ENZA* attempt when he was truly fearful for survival, he must have been doing some hard thinking. If they came through this, what would be his next challenge?

He was 46 and a more settled family life with his growing children was top priority. For him, the Trophée Jules Verne represented the pinnacle of his long-distance racing career, his greatest achievement as a sailor. There were to be no more mad dashes around the globe.

But there was also the matter of the America's Cup. *There was unfinished business.*

Was it possible that little New Zealand could ever take on the giants of the sailing world and actually *win* the 'Auld Mug'? Could the Kiwis ever beat the mighty, ruthless, massively well-funded Americans? Or the stylish, always unpredictable Italians? The daring, always dangerous French? Those tough, never-say-die Aussies from across the ditch?

Did he still have the competitive edge to want to be part of that?

We need to go back a few years here, to the first New Zealand attempts to win the America's Cup, happening while Peter was totally engrossed in his Whitbread campaigns.

At the 1986–87 America's Cup in Fremantle, New Zealand's first attempt for the trophy, New Zealand made it through the preliminary rounds to the Louis Vuitton challenger final, where they were defeated by the American Dennis Connor. In 1988 a radical New Zealand 'Big Boat' again took on Dennis Connor, both on the waters off San Diego and in the law courts — eventually and expensively losing in both arenas.

In 1992 New Zealand was gearing up for a third crack off San Diego. At that stage Peter was fresh from his *Steinlager 2* triumph and not particularly interested in round-the-buoys America's Cup yachting. But the New Zealand campaign, funded by businessmen Sir Michael Fay and David Richwhite (on their third and final attempt), needed a strong leader and Peter agreed to come in as project manager.

It was his first job in a purely managerial role, and not a happy one. He was promised complete control, but this never happened. His contribution could only be too little, and too late.

The New Zealand boat *NZL20* progressed all the way to the final of the Louis Vuitton Cup, but lost to the Italians 5-3.

Peter with Sir Michael Fay (to his left), both wearing the traditional korowai (Maori cloak), arriving for an America's Cup dawn ceremony at the San Diego Yacht Club, January 1992.

Peter did what he could through the disappointment and bitter legal battles over New Zealand's controversial bowsprit. In the end he couldn't get out of San Diego quick enough to prepare *ENZA* for the Trophée Jules Verne attempt.

At the same time, leaving San Diego, he had decided in his own mind that the America's Cup was winnable. 'Peel away the cloak and dagger stuff and it was just another yacht race with

The America's Cup

The America's Cup is the oldest trophy in international sport. It was named not for the country, as is often thought, but actually for a schooner named *America*, which defeated an English challenger in a race held around the Isle of Wight in England in 1851.

The iconic Auld Mug, an ornate silver trophy donated by the Royal Yacht Squadron, is among the world's most sought-after sporting trophies. Traditionally the match races around a laid-out course are fought between yachts representing two yacht clubs, the Defender and the Challenger. The New York Yacht Club held the trophy for 132 years until defeated in 1983 by a boat called *Australia II* representing the Royal Perth Yacht Club. It was the longest winning streak in any sport.

Until 1967, challengers for the America's Cup were always British yachts, with races between only the two contestants. In 1970, however, there was more than one potential challenger so a preliminary regatta was held to find the challenging boat. From 1983 to 2007 this was known as the Louis Vuitton Cup.

The type of yachts used for the event has changed dramatically over the decades. For the first hundred years the yachts were huge, especially the majestic J-class of the 1930s, which were 120-feet (36 metres) or more in length. Later, rules were changed to allow smaller, less costly boats like the famous 12-metre boats and more recently the International America's Cup class.

Until 2010 the races have been between monohull yachts. The best-of-three regatta in Valencia, Spain, in 2010 allowed multihulls for the first time, with the American challenger *BMW Oracle Racing* defeating the Swiss defender *Alinghi*. The 2013 America's Cup off San Francisco, California, will be raced between catamarans.

similar needs to any other long-term campaign that must have the right people if it is to succeed,' he wrote.

At the eleventh hour, just before entries closed, Pippa visited the Blakes' local bank manager and wrote out the hefty $US75,000 cheque required to accompany an official challenge (Peter was at sea taking delivery of *ENZA* from America). This commitment required Peter and Pippa to mortgage their house in Emsworth.

With the backing of the Royal New Zealand Yacht Squadron in Auckland, the challenge for 1995 was delivered. Team New Zealand was born.

Name, club, entry fee — all were ticked off. The task was to find a sponsor, or more likely, multiple sponsors, and the right sailors, designers and managers who, working together, could make their dream come true.

The required $30 million (minimum) did not come easy, especially when the Minister for Sport announced without warning that the government was withdrawing its NZ$4 million dollar promise to the campaign.

In fact it took many, many months of hard negotiating before a sponsorship family was put together and Team New Zealand was able to commit to the challenge. On board were Peter's previous sponsors Steinlager and ENZA, plus Toyota, Lotto and Television New Zealand (TVNZ).

He decided in his own mind that the America's Cup was winnable.

The complicated design work started. Boat-builders, riggers and sailmakers in Auckland were lined up. Peter's management team evolved into departments for design and testing, boat-building and shore work, rigs, sailing, administration and communication. Peter kept an overview as syndicate head.

Several decisions were made that are now thought to have been key to New Zealand's very unlikely success. These were the recruitment of the superb match-racing helmsman Russell Coutts as skipper, the decision to build two boats, and Coutts' decision to ask Peter to join the race crew.

As the first race for the Louis Vuitton regatta in San Diego drew closer, international media interest in New Zealand's two comparatively narrow black boats intensified. Which was faster: *NZL38*, which would go on to win 17 of her 18 Louis Vuitton races? Or could it be *NZL32*, dubbed *Black Magic* and kept as a closely guarded secret to race the America's Cup series itself?

Leading the charge, New Zealand had two of the most revered yachtsmen in the world; on the boat, Russell Coutts, Olympic gold medalist and winner of multiple world championships in various classes; off the boat, acting as campaign head, the great long-distance sailor Peter Blake. They, and all their hand-picked crew, staff and consultants, became a close-knit and formidable team.

The benefits of having Peter in *Black Magic*'s crew soon became apparent. Being in the thick of the action put a spring in his step! He could easily bridge any communication gap, should it occur, between race crew and shore staff, simply by hearing of any potential problems first-hand. His position on the boat required him to trim the mainsail, employing winches to adjust the sail for its best 'set'. Being at the back, close to the helmsman, he was right in the action, part of the decision-making.

It was a role he knew well, but the physical demands would take a toll on Peter's 47-year-old elbows. During the series he spent considerable time on the team physiotherapist's treatment table. The media interest grew ever greater, particularly as the Red Socks campaign began to grip the New Zealand public's imagination.

America's Cup racing is fierce: American challenger Stars & Stripes *crosses ahead of the Australian defender* Kookaburra 3. *New Zealand's* Kiwi Magic KZ-7 *made a huge impression in this 1987 regatta.*

Lucky Red Socks

'Pete's Lucky Socks' wasn't a new concept. Most sailors have their superstitions and in the case of the Blake family it was tradition for Pippa to present Peter with a pair of bright ski socks before a race, to be dug out whenever the crew needed a morale boost, something extra besides their skill and good weather.

On the *Steinlager 2* race the socks were multi-coloured and fluorescent, and first saw light on the yacht after rounding Cape Horn with Grant Dalton's *Fisher & Paykel* keeping up the pressure only a few miles behind.

On Christmas Eve 1994, in San Diego, Pippa's chosen socks were red, and posh ones at that: designer brand Ralph Lauren. Peter decided to wear them for the first race in the Louis Vuitton series. 'We won,' recalls Peter, 'so I decided the socks were lucky and wore red socks throughout the campaign.' In fact, the only race that Team New Zealand lost in the entire campaign was the one against Australia where Peter, with a troublesome elbow, was not aboard wearing his red socks. Pippa recalls that, 'overnight the outcry was "Get Blake back on the boat with his lucky red socks!" With Peter back aboard the next day, they never lost another race.'

It wasn't just luck the Lucky Red Socks were generating. A bright young marketer from TVNZ had suggested that they could be used to front a fundraising campaign. Team New Zealand's ability to buy

Children in Tibet wearing Lucky Red Socks.

Many businesses also supported the Red Socks campaign.

necessary new sails and gear for the crucial last round of racing was looking decidedly grim.

No-one anticipated the Red Socks phenomenon. More than $100,000 was raised, but it wasn't just money. New Zealand went into a Red Socks frenzy, so intense that the country's knitting mills struggled to meet the demand. The Governor General wore them. The prime minister and other politicians wore them. On stage for concerts, the Auckland Philharmonia Orchestra showed theirs off under their evening dress. Animals, even the elephant at the Auckland Zoo, wore red.

Ordinary Kiwis up and down the country were seen 'socked up' in schools, factories, supermarkets and on commuter buses, showing their support to the boys in San Diego. In fact, red socks became a recognised symbol for 'Kiwi spirit'.

It was David versus Goliath, one of the world's smaller nations up against the mightiest. But this time, as had always been the case, it wasn't a question of who had the most money or the weight of history behind them. Writing about his experience, Peter concluded that:

Team New Zealand's challenge was a statement about the determination and ability of a small country. I believe we caught the Americans at a time when they were confident that they would win purely because the Cup had only been taken away from them once [by Australia in 1983] in 144 years. But they hadn't taken into consideration the expertise and the enormous will to win that exists in New Zealand, as well as the vast amount of experience acquired in all types of competitive sailing over the years.

The crew on Young America *were always good sports when we raced them. But I think they soon knew that it would take a miracle to stop our black yacht from achieving the unthinkable.* (Adventurer, p. 132)

The miracle was *Black Magic*, her designers, builders and sailors. She saw off all the Louis Vuitton challengers with only the loss of one single (sockless) race, and then trounced one of the most famous skippers in America's Cup history, Dennis Connor, 5–0.

The last race was won on Mothers' Day in New Zealand, 13 May 1995. Television and radio broadcast the good news to the nation. Feelings ranged from jubilation to relief to incredulity! The winning moments of the last race were replayed over and over, with sailing commentator Peter Montgomery beside himself with excitement.

'The America's Cup is now New Zealand's cup!'

Black Magic, NZL32 *on her way to victory.*

Despite the many thousands of telegrams and messages they received in San Diego, nothing prepared Peter and his team for the reception that greeted them in Auckland. From the window of an Air New Zealand jumbo with an America's Cup painted on the outside, the team got a hint of what was in store. To their right was a huge red hot-air balloon with a giant, 60-foot (18 metre) sock hanging from it. On the runway fire tenders were lined up to greet the aircraft. At the door of the plane Peter Blake and Russell Coutts held aloft the priceless America's Cup. What a moment!

There were countless throngs at the airport, and more thousands lining the streets into the city holding red-pawed dogs and cats aloft as the Team New Zealand coaches passed. But what greeted the team in Auckland city was pandemonium. Nothing like it has been seen before or since, not even at the 2011 Rugby World Cup celebrations, supporting Peter's claim in his book *Adventurer* that, as baseball is in America or football in Europe, so sailing is for New Zealanders.

In May 1995 this was true, as it would be again in 2000.

Ticker-tape, flowers and confetti rained down as the parade of vehicles carrying Cup and crew proceeded up Queen Street, where hundreds of thousands of people had gathered to welcome the returning heroes. Red socks were everywhere.

This was the day, perhaps, that hoisted Peter in the eyes of the nation into that small pantheon of true national heroes: Sir Edmund Hillary, Bruce Maclaren, Jack Lovelock, Sir Peter Snell and Sir Murray Halberg. It was New Zealand's biggest day since Hillary stood on top of Everest in 1953, declared the Governor-General, Dame Catherine Tizard.

The celebrations were not only in Auckland. True to form, Peter and his crew wanted to share their success with all the country. Official civic welcomes and parades, no less ecstatic, were held in Wellington, Christchurch and Dunedin. From their aircraft approaching Dunedin, they were astonished to see on the

'The America's Cup is now New Zealand's Cup!'

Wellington marked the 1995 America's Cup victory with its front page coverage of the victory parade attended by around 250,000 people. Peter and Team New Zealand then attended Prime Minister Jim Bolger's official welcome at Parliament.

ground below an enormous red sock created by workers at the Roslyn Woollen Mills, and the workers sporting red t-shirts and of course, on their feet, lucky socks. Even sheep got in on the act. Pippa recalls that driving in from the airport, they saw 'the most extraordinary sight: farmers had dipped their entire flocks of sheep into red dye!'

In Wellington Peter received a call from an official at the Department of Internal Affairs, advising him that in the next Queen's Birthday Honours' list he would be getting a knighthood. He would receive this third Queen's honour at Government House, where Dame Catherine would lightly touch his left shoulder with a ceremonial sword and say 'Arise, Sir Peter.'

Blue Water, Black Magic

NZL32 Black Magic 1 was the first boat built in Auckland for the 1995 America's Cup challenge. Her sister ship, *NZL38 Black Magic 2*, won the Louis Vuitton Challenge series 5–1, but the America's Cup regatta itself was won by *NZL32 Black Magic 1*.

Instead of using a single designer, Team New Zealand created a design team of, principally, Doug Peterson, Laurie Davidson and Tom Schnackenberg, along with ten others. Both yachts were built of carbon fibre by a team led by Tim Gurr at McMullen & Wing, Auckland, in 1993.

When unveiled the yachts were regarded as radical designs within the America's Cup rules. Both were significantly narrower than the yachts that contested the 1992 America's Cup, and featured keels with a torpedo-shaped bulb, which attracted much interest and speculation. Initially judged by rivals as being slow, both yachts' performances in the two regattas soon showed otherwise. Out of an exhausting programme of 23 races, they lost only one.

After the regatta, *NZL32 Black Magic 1* was shipped back to New Zealand and, with the support of the Blake family, was gifted to the Museum of New Zealand Te Papa Tongarewa. In 2009, *Black Magic 1* became the centrepiece of a permanent exhibition at the Voyager New Zealand Maritime Museum in Auckland, created as an enduring tribute to the life, achievements and memory of Sir Peter Blake. It was a joint project of the Voyager Maritime Museum and Te Papa, with significant investment from the New Zealand Government and Auckland City Council.

The exhibition, in a redeveloped wing of the museum on Hobson Wharf, was designed by New Zealand architect Pete Bossley. Besides displaying *Black Magic*, the exhibition portrays Sir Peter's Whitbread Round-the-World, Trophée Jules Verne and America's Cup campaigns. It also profiles other key designers, sailors and contributors to New Zealand's boating industry. The exhibition also has interactive features designed to appeal to young people and families, engaging them in experiences exploring the elements of leadership, the part played by failure, and Sir Peter's well-known maxim that, 'If something's not hard, it's not worth doing.'

Brothers Peter and Tony Blake out for a spin on the Waitemata Harbour in Peter's Z-class Tango.

The Blake family ketch, Ladybird.

Steinlager 2 *pushes her way through the typically choppy waters churned up by spectator boats attending a Whitbread Round-the-World race start.*

The escort fleet now left behind, Steinlager's *crew settle to trimming the sails.*

Co-skippers Peter Blake and Robin Knox-Johnston aboard Enza New Zealand *for their first Trophée Jules Verne attempt, 1992.*

Voyagers (ex-trainees) on the youth development ship Spirit of New Zealand *proudly display their red socks.*

The sweetest victory! Peter, Russell Coutts and the crew of Black Magic *have just been given the America's Cup by the Commodore of the San Diego Yacht Club, May 1995.*

Peter, Russell Coutts and the America's Cup are surrounded by ecstatic crowds at Auckland's tickertape victory parade, February 2000.

'Arise, Sir Peter.' Governor General Dame Catherine Tizard creates a new sporting knight, Sir Peter Blake.

Seamaster, *dwarfed by the magnificence of the Antarctic icescape.*

Seamaster *in the Antarctic.*

Peter in the Amazon with his beloved Seamaster.

Peter aboard his last boat, Seamaster.

Lady Pippa Blake, on Peter's behalf, receives the Olympic Order from King Constantine of Greece at the Emsworth Sailing Club, England.

10

'The America's Cup is *still* New Zealand's Cup!'

When an America's Cup is won, the winning team doesn't just take home a magnificent piece of silverware. It also takes on the obligation to organise and host the next Cup regatta.

From the moment *Black Magic* crossed the finishing line and Peter Montgomery announced to the world that 'The America's Cup is now New Zealand's Cup!', Aucklanders knew that they were going to give the biggest party in the city's history. Not only that, 2000 Millennium celebrations were also being planned.

Fun and hugely challenging, yes, but Peter knew it was going to be even harder to *defend* the Cup than it had been to challenge for it. New Zealand was only the second country to wrest the Cup away from the Americans in 144 years. Australia, which had won in 1983, had not been able to win a second time in Fremantle in 1988, and the Cup had returned to America. Could tiny New Zealand do the unimaginable and win a second time?

It was this challenge that appealed to Peter. Five years later he would tell Pippa that he wished he'd moved on to other things in 1995. But at the time the prospect of leading another campaign in his home city seemed hugely compelling.

The 1995 victory, he said, 'was only a beginning. We had achieved one goal, but now there is a new one. Goal setting is very important and unless the goal is a difficult one, it is hardly worth bothering about. At Team New Zealand, we are in no doubt that we face an extremely difficult goal. The America's Cup ... has never been successfully defended outside of the US. Our job is to keep it here for as long as possible.'

Commitments had been made to sponsors and to the public, emphasising the benefits to the country and to Auckland that would result if an America's Cup regatta was to be held there.

Whatever the outcome in 2000, Peter made it clear that he would be moving on from Team New Zealand. The future of the world's oceans would become his focus.

Peter had strong views on what the Auckland regatta would offer challenging nations, and how it would be different and better than any that had gone before. It would be a fair contest, he announced. 'There will be no shifting of the rules. If they don't want to play by the book, they should not bother to come at all.' He was enormously excited about the impact the whole regatta and a new America's Cup village would have on his beloved Waitemata Harbour and the waterfront area of the city. His vision was for Aucklanders and the many expected visitors from overseas to be able to enjoy the party atmosphere fully. This would best be achieved by having the syndicates gathered together in a central location.

It was hard work, involving politicians, planners, lawyers, business interests and ordinary citizens, but soon plans were being developed to create 'Syndicate Row', with all the teams' sheds lined up on one side of the Viaduct Basin. An area of the waterfront that had suffered decades of neglect would be transformed into a bright new public space.

Peter was not the only major player, of course, but he was hugely influential in what was planned and achieved. His old friend Sir Tom Clark described him as 'a shaggy-haired sheepdog, barking and snapping at their heels' as he herded the various players into the fold.

At the same time, Team New Zealand was being reorganised to defend 'New Zealand's Cup'. Many of the key

Peter Blake received two honorary doctorates; a Doctor of Commerce from Massey University in 1999 and an Honorary Doctorate from the Auckland University of Technology (AUT) in 2000.

people involved in the 1995 success committed themselves to the team. The sponsorship family was extended. For the next four years the public assumed that all was going well and that the Cup defence was in the best possible hands of Sir Peter Blake, Russell Coutts and the major players from 1995. Team New Zealand's smart new black boat, *NZL60*, was unveiled, and frequently seen being towed out of the harbour for training spins in the inner Hauraki Gulf area, where the races would take place.

The public heard about the massive amounts of money and effort being committed to campaigns by 11 entrants from seven countries, and warmly welcomed their teams as they took up residence in the city. Their sleek boats could also be seen out daily, for intensive crew training on the harbour and gulf.

The Millennium was coming and the America's Cup would be raced over the summer of 1999–2000. What a great party it was going to be! The Viaduct Basin was transformed into the buzzing waterfront area long dreamed of by Aucklanders.

The Millennium party came and went and the Louis Vuitton races were sailed. Italy's *Luna Rossa* beat *AmericaOne* to emerge as the popular challenger.

With excitement for the first cup race at fever pitch, New Zealand's faith in Team New Zealand was justified when the new

Black Magic NZL60 pulled ahead on the very first leg, and went on to win the series 5–0. *Luna Rossa* had no answer to the clever hull design, better sails, a stronger mast, superb crew work and an innovative sound system giving skipper Russell Coutts the ability to speak to his crew through smart little earpieces rather than shout orders.

'The America's Cup is *still* New Zealand's Cup,' screamed Peter Montgomery in the dying moments of the last race.

Once again, New Zealand went berserk. Hundreds of thousands of people, perhaps even more than in 1995, attended the ticker-tape parade up Queen Street to Aotea Square. Prime Minister Helen Clark arranged for an Air Force aircraft to do a victory lap over Auckland then fly the crew to victory parades and ceremonies in southern cities.

Peter with his family on board Black Magic *just after she crossed the line in San Diego to win the America's Cup. It's said 95% of New Zealand's population watched the fifth and last race live on television.*

To the public, Team New Zealand's win was due to brilliant designers and boat-builders, to the world's best sailors, and, in Sir Peter Blake and his team, the best management. Sadly, it gradually became known that for Peter and the loyal team at Team New Zealand, the four years of preparation had been very difficult.

Increasingly, says Pippa, 'the defence became not so much about sailing but about power, personal politics and money … He tussled with all this, and it stressed him in a way that the toughest sailing had never stressed him.'

She remembers it as a time of high pressure, worry and separation. Peter was mostly in Auckland, with James attending an Auckland boys' school, but Sarah-Jane remained at boarding school in England and for a time Pippa carried on at Emsworth. The family would get together at school holidays for skiing, or meet up in England to go cruising in Scotland's outer islands or the Mediterranean on a boat called *Archangel* that Peter had quietly purchased after San Diego.

As the 2000 defence drew nearer, pressure mounted. To cope, Peter would go paddling in a kayak, or treasure quiet moments with the children or a cup of tea with his elderly mother. 'He protected us from most of it,' recalls Pippa, 'didn't really want to bring that baggage home … He never held grievances. He'd just get on with it and leave it all behind him. I know he offered to resign on at least a couple of occasions when the stress of it all was really getting to him. He really did want to leave. But it was for New Zealand and he didn't want to let anyone down. He would see it through … '

Seeing it through meant some of the penalties of fame. A death-threat letter aimed at the children was enough for Peter to agree to six security guards being camped in the Blake family garage. Two security guards accompanied him to work every day, while a female guard accompanied Pippa and Sarah-Jane whenever they went out. 'It was over the top and not great for

Back at the dock, just given the America's Cup to hold, Peter and his victorious crew celebrate a very special moment.

family, so they were not happy times,' recalls Pippa.

Despite all these undercurrents unknown to the public, Team New Zealand won the series comprehensively and Sir Peter accompanied the silver America's Cup on a second triumphant ticker-tape parade up Queen Street. He must have felt huge relief. He had done his very best to keep the Cup in New Zealand. Job done, sorted.

Now he was free to do what he had always said he would after the Cup; move on to where his passion and his dreams now lay.

It can't have been any pleasure to him when he heard only a few months later that Team New Zealand had lost five of its key members. They would be sailing on a Swiss boat at the next America's Cup in 2003.

There, in Auckland, Team New Zealand's *NZL82* suffered multiple gear failures in the first race and went on to a sad 5–0 defeat at the hands of the Swiss-based challenger *Alinghi*.

'The America's Cup is *still* New Zealand's Cup!'

Peter Blake and Russell Coutts present the America's Cup to the huge crowds gathered in Wellington, May 1995.

What is leadership?

Mark Orams was a crew member on *Steinlager 2* and worked for Team New Zealand and blakexpeditions. In his book *Blake: Leader* he shares thoughts and stories about what constitutes leadership. Following is a summary of some of the comments Orams makes in his book.

- As a skipper Peter didn't merely give orders and supervise. When a job needed doing, especially in terrible conditions, he'd get in beside his crew and lend a hand (p. 24). Peter led by example. Great leadership is about deeds not words.
- Peter wasn't afraid to fail (p. 34). He believed the greatest failure is to have a great dream and not pursue it. Peter was a dreamer, but what made him different was that he had the guts, confidence and burning desire to turn those dreams into reality. He said, 'Giving it a try is much better than sitting back and worrying what people might think if we fail ... if you're not prepared to make a mistake, well, you're not going to make anything.' (p. 70)

- Little courtesies mean much. After every order, no matter how terse or how tense the situation, without fail, Peter added, 'Please.' And when the particular crisis was over: 'Nice work, guys, well done. Thanks very much.' (p. 59)
- Decisions, even trivial ones, can reflect a team culture. It was agreed by the *Steinlager 2* crew that books were vital when people couldn't sleep. But books are heavy. They jointly decided to take only one paperback each, to be shared around, and to remove the covers to save weight. Ridiculous? Maybe, but it demonstrated the crew's understanding that lots of little things added up to a big advantage, and reflected the general 'no-compromise' culture that won them the race. (p. 60)
- No one person in a team is too big for any job. *Any* job. Mark Orams held a first-class honours degree in resource management. His first job on *Steinlager 2* was to be in charge of keeping the bilges and the toilets clean! However, there was a 15-day roster to do the job and *everyone* did it, including the skipper. (p. 61)
- Humour is important in teams (p. 64). Peter loved nothing better than to throw his head back and laugh. Humour could be useful too. Peter's crews knew of the 'Dick of the Day' tradition on his boats. Around sundown, perhaps at a time of changing watches, the crew would recall something stupid or annoying that had happened during the day. A lot of banter would follow and a 'winner' was agreed. Fun, but it also got things out in the open in a safe manner. It was a good way to release tension.
- To the question, 'What makes a good leader?' Peter's answer was, 'The ability to listen.' (p. 76)
- When asked what makes a team compatible, he said, 'The critical factor is the harmony of the team and the chemistry. Of course you have to have the expertise in camp — you can't run without having the people who know what they are doing — but if people don't get on together, if they aren't compatible, you might as well pack your tent up and go home because it isn't going to work.' (p. 170)

- On doing your best: 'As long as you know deep inside that you've done the best you possibly can, whether you've actually won or come second, as long as you can look yourself in the mirror and say "I couldn't have done it any better", that's all I can ever ask of anybody.' (p. 171)

* Page numbers refer to the fuller accounts in Oram's book.

11
Ambassador for the environment

For more than 30 years, since his first passage to Tonga as a teenager on *Ladybird*, Peter's natural home had been the world's oceans. After the epic round-world trip in *ENZA*, no sailor in history had ever personally amassed more sea miles.

Now 52, with his competitive sailing days behind him, Peter was moving back to make his base with the family in Emsworth. He was also itching to move into a new phase of his career. This phase would not be about speed, about winning races or silver cups. It would be about the great oceans that had given him so much pleasure.

During his Whitbread and *ENZA* voyages, Peter had always had time to watch the albatrosses and shearwaters circling above, the elegant flying fish skipping along the surface in the tropics, and the pods of whales and dolphins. Perhaps, he'd thought during his final Whitbread races, there were fewer albatrosses in the Southern Ocean? Now he was reading that 40,000 albatrosses were being caught every year by long-lines and driftnets. If everything he was reading about the increasing pollution of the oceans and places like the Antarctic was even half true, then this was a terrible state of affairs.

He decided that now was the time to do something. He would use his international profile and his ability to find sponsors and interest the media. He had enough money to provide for his family and to purchase the sort of boat he had in mind for his work. He had friends and contacts all over the world who were supportive of his plan. He would become an ambassador for the environment.

But he wasn't destined to achieve this dream with his first attempt. In 1997 Peter had been approached by the Cousteau Society to meet its founder, the legendary Jacques-Yves Cousteau. Through his television programmes, Cousteau was known world-wide as an explorer, ecologist, filmmaker, scientist, photographer, author and researcher. Now 87, he was looking for someone of like mind to continue his work. But before he and Peter could meet, Cousteau died. The Society, headed by his widow Francine, continued talks with Peter. A year or so on Peter took a short break from the America's Cup to lead a joint UNESCO-Cousteau expedition on the vessel *Alcyone*. These, penetrating deep into Asia, were fascinating new waterways for Peter: the Black Sea and the Don and Volga rivers into Azerbaijan.

However, the *Alcyone* wasn't the right vessel for the sort of Arctic and Antarctic exploration that Peter had in mind. To continue the Cousteau Society's work he felt two or three vessels would be desirable. He quietly started a search. He flew to France to see *Antarctica*, which was moored in a small port on the Atlantic coast. Peter had previously crossed tacks mid-ocean with *Antarctica* when he was roaring through the Southern Ocean on *ENZA*, skirting the Antarctic Circle. They'd even talked on their radios. She was a 118-foot (36-metre) schooner, built of reinforced aluminium for polar sea exploration. Just back from a charter to Iceland,

Peter, with the UNESCO special flag for the World Year of the Water, aboard the Cousteau boat Alcyone *on the Don Canal, Russia, 1998.*

she was to Peter, just perfect! He really loved that boat, Pippa recalls, ' ... not exactly pretty but well thought through and absolutely purposeful. Peter was never swayed by luxury. Give him functional every time.'

Antarctica was purchased, provisioned and sailed by friends out to New Zealand. Tied up in Auckland's Viaduct Basin alongside visiting glamorous megayachts gathered for the America's Cup, she was a visible, if rather ungainly, public statement of Peter's intentions once the Cup was over. Sadly, the partnership with the Cousteau Society did not eventuate. Discussions with Madame Cousteau revealed differences over funding and Peter's role.

The next question was, could he proceed under his own name? The answer from his business associates and close friends was a clear 'yes!' A five-year plan for blakexpeditions was then drawn up.

In *Antarctica*, Peter and crews would journey to parts of the world that were considered ecologically threatened. He and his team would report on the effects of global warming, pollution and exploitation. First would be a trip to Antarctica itself to report on any retreat of the south polar ice shelf. Following that would be a journey to Brazil and Venezuela to venture 1400 miles (2253 kilometres) up the Amazon and Negro rivers. They would look for the impacts of changing weather patterns, increased population, over-fishing and rapidly diminishing forests. After that they would go to the Pacific region to the Galapagos, China's Yangtze River, Japan's coral reefs and Australia's Great Barrier Reef, followed by a circumnavigation of Antarctica and a journey around the Mediterranean and up the Nile and down the Ganges River.

Fired up, Peter had no difficulty finding an initial sponsor: the famous Swiss watch company Omega. Happy with their association with Peter and Team New Zealand since 1995, they signed up almost immediately. *Antarctica* became *Seamaster*.

In November 2000, refurbished and provisioned for 15 people, *Seamaster* left the Waitemata on her first great adventure. Peter

The powerful blakeexpeditions vessel, Seamaster.

writes during their first Southern Ocean gale, compared to his racing yachts, 'being on *Seamaster* is like being on an aircraft carrier. At times she was right on the top of a crest of breaking, foaming white water and it seemed as though the bow of our vessel was in the air on one side of the crest, while the stern was in the air on the other. Most times, however, the waves went harmlessly underneath.'

His logs on the voyage are full of observations about the birdlife and the sea states. He acknowledged that sailing across an ocean probably means different things to different people.

'Generally, though, it makes people appreciate how large the oceans are, how much water there is, and also how much life there is. It isn't just a great, empty expanse of only wind and waves ... For me, after racing past so many times, to now be able to stop and look at what I have only seen fleetingly through binoculars, fills a void.'

In Ushuaia, on the southern tip of Argentina, South America, Peter was joined first by son James for Christmas and a short time later, by Pippa and Sarah-Jane. The family enjoyed a magical 'summer' holiday cruising among the many islands of

In the deep south: Peter and penguins.

the Beagle Channel and Tierra del Fuego. Despite the freezing temperatures, Peter and James donned wetsuits and went diving. Then, with the family back to school and work, it was on to Antarctica, reporting on the disturbing changes to the sea ice, melting quicker than ever before recorded.

Peter was overwhelmed by what was his first leisurely, real Antarctic experience, as most people are. He wrote, 'You suddenly realise that you are part of something far greater, more magnificent and intricate, and more fragile than you ever imagined. You suddenly understand that the environment must be appreciated and nurtured for all the right reasons, that it is what makes this planet of ours different to anything in the known solar system.'

Through a satellite link to a United Nations conference of environment ministers from more than 80 countries gathered in Nairobi, he was able to give one of his first formal messages in his new role.

> *To describe what we have found over the past few days and weeks, to be here on* Seamaster *on a piece of sea that no one has ever been on before (because it*

> *is normally frozen) really brings home what is actually happening to the ice ... It is now going to be, more and more, up to individuals who will accept nothing less than what is needed to enable nature to accommodate our presence on the planet.*
>
> *That is the reason for blakexpeditions and what we are doing ... and we are using all of the modern communications technologies to do so.* (Sir Peter Blake: An Amazing Life, *p. 384*)

Peter was clearly in his element. He sent out daily website offerings with descriptions of wildlife and the risky territory he and his team were exploring. Leaving the South Shetlands area in March, *Seamaster* was caught trying to find a passage through pack ice and the driving sleet of a full Southern Ocean gale. She was lucky to escape. Although he'd raced often enough through these latitudes, Peter wrote, 'I have never had a night like that one ... *Seamaster* really came into her own. Only equivalent ice-breakers would have attempted such a passage.'

After reprovisioning in Ushuaia, their next stop was the

Seamaster's *crew photographed their ship against many grand Antarctic landscapes.*

Amazon, 4000 miles (6437 kilometres) to the north. This journey took five months and included stops in Buenos Aires and Rio de Janerio to check the boat over and make her more suitable for a nearly 3000 mile (4828 kilometre) voyage in the tropical heat of the Amazon and Negro rivers. Fridges, insect nets, awnings, fans and a special water purification unit were loaded aboard.

Peter's ambassadorial role was gathering momentum. He flew back to New Zealand where he was appointed a Special Envoy for the United Nations Environment Programme. He went to England to complete two television documentaries about his Antarctic expedition. Then back to Buenos Aires for some filming for sponsor Omega, to London to set up arrangements for more documentaries, then back to rejoin *Seamaster*.

It was exhausting, but he was loving every minute of it. Sarah-Jane shared some of the voyaging as *Seamaster* worked her way north. When *Seamaster* had navigated her way to the mouth of the Amazon and then was a good way up the Rio Negro, Pippa joined Peter for a month. She had nursed a dream of visiting the Amazon since childhood and was determined to seize this opportunity, however long and difficult the journey to join *Seamaster*. It was the happiest of times for both as they combined his passion for the environment with Pippa's passion for art. At last, even though they knew they would always have long periods apart, their lives really seemed to be in harmony.

Peter continued writing his daily websites and carrying out skipper duties, and Pippa sketched and painted. In oppressive heat they'd go canoeing, spotting giant otters and alligators, visit little riverside settlements or just listen to the squawks of parrots and toucans. Pippa marvelled that 'we were a thousand miles from the open ocean and there we were in the middle of the Amazon rainforest.'

In mid-November, *Seamaster* hosted a visit from the New Zealand Prime Minister, Helen Clark, and an entourage of nine. Pippa observed of the prime minister that she 'shared

[Peter's] passion for making a difference.' The prime minister and two senior diplomats were given bunks, but the other six had to sleep in hammocks strung up on deck. Peter took the party canoeing and the ship's Brazilian cook prepared a magnificent feast. After dark they went on to a sandbank, creeping around with torches to look for alligators' eyes gleaming in the dark. The Prime Minister and party left, and on 30 November, Pippa farewelled *Seamaster*, planning to see Peter in three weeks. She would take the children to join Peter in the Caribbean for a joyful Christmas holiday.

Making friends with children from river villages.

On 5 December *Seamaster* was approaching the town of Macapá, still on the Rio Negro. Peter made his last entry in his logbook for the night.

> *The top of the environmental awareness mountain we are endeavouring to climb may be out of sight through the clouds right now. But to win, you first have to believe you can do it. You have to be passionate about it. You have to really 'want' the result — even if this means years of hard work.*
>
> *The hardest part of any project is to begin.*
>
> *We have begun. We are under way. We have a passion. We want to make a difference ...* (Sir Peter Blake: An Amazing Life, *p. 402*)

December 6 began like any other day. Peter decided to move *Seamaster* several miles downstream to anchor about 200 metres

Peter takes a bus trip with a young fan during the Amazon adventure.

off the small village of Fazendinha. There she would be less conspicuous; Macapá had a reputation for 'river rats', local gangs that occasionally raided visiting vessels. Peter and some of the crew went ashore, returning at sunset.

Relaxing in the cockpit over dinner, his crew noticed his high spirits and his excitement about blakexpeditions' terrific start. Two television documentaries were going to air around the world, with another two in preparation and the possibility of the BBC coming aboard as a partner. The website was reaching schools and supportive individuals all over the world. He talked of blakexpeditions owning two or three *Seamasters* and having the ability to respond quickly to environmental events.

Sometime after 10, around the time when a skipper might be going to write up the day in his logbook before retiring, the relaxed *Seamaster* crew were suddenly confronted by eight armed intruders, demanding that they hand over watches and money.

In the ensuing fracas, while trying to defend his crew, Peter was shot and killed. The gang of river rats quickly made their escape, stealing one of *Seamaster*'s tenders.

Their haul of loot was a few watches.

Peter's distraught crew continued attempts to resuscitate him for an hour, until the emergency team that eventually turned up confirmed that nothing could be done. Peter was two months past his 53rd birthday. News of his death trying to protect his crew made shocking headlines around the world, no more so than in his own country. Many people felt that his death robbed New Zealand of a future governor-general, or the United Nations of a senior diplomat who would, in his lifetime, make his mark in global environmental politics.

Peter's body was flown back to England. On 14 December he was buried at a little church near his home in Emsworth. The funeral at the 11th-century Church of St Thomas à Becket was attended by more than a thousand people, including representatives of the royal family, United Nations, and the British and New Zealand governments. Former Blake crew members made the long journey from New Zealand to act as pallbearers, the last thing they could do for their skipper.

Inspiring the next generation of environmentalists.

An estimated 30,000 people crowded into the Auckland Domain for the memorial service held for Sir Peter Blake.

In the churchyard, Peter Blake's headstone, made of ancient Cumbrian green slate chosen by Pippa, bears the inscription:

Sir Peter Blake KBE
1948 to 2001
Yachtsman and adventurer
of New Zealand
and of
Emsworth

On the reverse is Peter's favourite poem, John Masefield's *Sea Fever*, which begins: 'I must down to the sea again, to the lonely sea and sky, and all I ask is a tall ship and a star to steer her by ... ' Visitors find the grave easily because of the small tributes placed there: a New Zealand flag or two, toy kiwi, flowers and several pairs of red socks.

In New Zealand, two days before Christmas, more than 30,000 people gathered for a memorial service on the grassy slopes of the Auckland Domain, overlooking the Waitemata Harbour. It was a state occasion attended by Governor-General Dame Silvia Cartwright, Prime Minister Helen Clark and Sir Hugh Kawharu representing Auckland's largest iwi, Ngati Whatua. From Brazil came Mr Lars Grael, the National Secretary of Sports, representing President Fernando Henrique Cardoso.

'Our small nation went into shock,' Helen Clark told the gathering. 'Peter Blake was a living legend. As an outstanding sailor, he had brought great honour and fame to New Zealand. His death was unthinkable.'

Later in the day, towards sunset, more than 8000 boats gathered in the Waitemata to take part in a 'sail-past' as a tribute to the boy from Bayswater who had once rowed around the Shoal Bay mangroves and roared across the harbour in his black-hulled Zeddie, whooping with joy.

The headstone of Sir Peter Blake's grave in Emsworth, England.

12

Epilogue

Peter's story, like that of all great men and women, does not end with his death.

In Brazil, eight men were found guilty of charges relating to murder. The two who used their guns were sentenced to prison terms of 36 and 35 years, later reduced slightly on appeal. The six others were jailed for terms ranging from four months to 32 years.

In New Zealand, Helen Clark welcomed the verdicts, saying that, 'the final sentence for these young men reflects the severity of the crimes they committed and I am satisfied that justice has been done in this case.'

In England, the coroner recorded a verdict of unlawful killing, stating, 'On that night Sir Peter Blake showed outstanding bravery in trying to protect his colleagues and the ship in what must have been for everyone terrifying circumstances. He was a great man.'

In the village of Emsworth, Pippa and their children received more than 3000 messages and very slowly rebuilt their lives. Invitations to accept honours on Peter's behalf came thick and fast.

Pippa had little previous experience in public speaking, but she learned quickly. In Johannesburg, she spoke to 600 delegates at the World Earth Summit. In New Zealand, accepting the New Zealand Sportsman of the Year Award, Pippa was astonished when the audience of 1200 rose to give her a standing ovation — a rare honour in that country. It was, she recalls, a tough night.

Tougher again was travelling to Monaco to receive Peter's Lifetime Achievement Award from the Laureus World Sports Academy. These are sport's Oscars, attended by a glittering crowd of top sportsmen and women from all over the world. Told that she and the children would not have to go up on stage, Pippa found herself and children being escorted by All Black Sean Fitzpatrick to the stage and invited by actor Sean Connery to speak! She held her children close and managed to get some words out. Of the ten Lifetime Achievement awards presented by the Laureas Academy, Peter is so far the only yachtsman.

Probably the most rare award was the Olympic Order, presented by King Constantine at the Emsworth Sailing Club. The highest award of the Olympic movement, it is sparingly given, very rarely ever to a non-Olympian. Peter is one of only three to be awarded posthumously since 1976.

One memorial that would have been dear to Peter's boyhood memories is the funding available to young members of his old sailing club in Emsworth, where he and Pippa first met. Grants are made for special tuition or costs involved in entering major yachting events.

In New Zealand, politicians and sports bodies debated how best to create a lasting memorial to Peter Blake. There were suggestions of statues and renaming the waterfront Viaduct Basin in his name. Efforts by Peter's business associates and friends to keep his name alive by continuing with *Seamaster* and blakexpeditions proved, without Peter's name and drive, to be unsustainable. The yacht was sold and renamed *Tara*.

Two major memorials were established in Auckland. The Voyager National Maritime Museum created a permanent exhibition as a tribute to Peter Blake's life, featuring as its centrepiece the legendary 1995 *Black Magic NZL32*. It was opened in 2009.

The Sir Peter Blake Medal is awarded annually and serves as recognition of the achievements of an outstanding New Zealander.

In 2004, the New Zealand government, supported by the Blake family, decided to give $3.8 million for a Sir Peter Blake Trust. Based in Auckland, the Trust would establish an ambitious programme of activities and awards 'to help New Zealanders make a positive difference for the planet through activities that encourage environmental awareness and action, and leadership development.'

Every year the Trust awards the Blake Medal to an outstanding New Zealand leader. These have included businessman Sir Stephen Tindall, scientist Sir Paul Callaghan and Olympic sportsman and philanthropist Sir Murray Halberg.

The Sir Peter Blake Emerging Leader awards are presented annually to six young people recognised as future leaders, while the Trust annually helps fund a young scientist or environmentalist to be a Youth Ambassador to the Antarctic. The Trust also organises its annual Leadership Week, the annual Youth EnviroLeaders' Forum, the Care for our Coast programme and Red Socks Day, when communities gather together to celebrate their leaders in whatever way they choose.

In 2012, 30 secondary school students took part in the first Blake expedition to the remote and seldom-visited Kermadec Islands, travelling aboard HMNZS *Canterbury*.

Children from Bayswater Primary School take part in the Care for our Coast programme.

Besides the work of the Trust, some yachting organisations have honoured Peter Blake. These include the Marine Education and Recreation Centre at Long Bay, north of Auckland, which after his death was renamed the Sir Peter Blake Marine Education and Recreation Centre. Each December the Torbay Sailing Club on Auckland's North Shore runs the Sir Peter Blake Memorial Torbay Youth Regatta (New Zealand's largest youth regatta) with the major award, the Sir Peter Blake Memorial Trophy, going to the outstanding young sailor.

Children find all sorts of amazing things on beach clean-ups!

The Sir Peter Blake Trophy is awarded by the North Harbour Club as the top award for talented local young people, while his old primary school, Bayswater Primary School, gives the Sir Peter Blake Young Environmentalists' Award to teams shining in environmental projects. The new school hall, built in 2003, was also named after their former pupil, Peter Blake.

> *The spirit of adventure never dies.*
> *At its best it is born in the support and sharing of a family or friends.*
> *It can manifest itself in the work of the painter, the playing of music or even the laughter of children.*
> *It does not have to be competitively top gun, either with others or strangely enough, even oneself.*
> *It can be inherited through example but never imposed. And when the shouting dies away perhaps the greatest reward for any adventurer is to see it quietly growing in the next generation.*
>
> *Sir Peter Blake*

Sir Peter Blake — honours and awards

Honours

1983	MBE, for services to yachting
1991	OBE, for services to yachting
1995	KBE (Knight Commander of the Civil Division of the Most Excellent Order of the British Empire), for services to yachting
	Inducted into the America's Cup Hall of Fame
1996	Fellow of the Royal Geographic Society
1999	D. Com., Massey University
2000	Honorary Doctorate, Auckland University of Technology
2001	Appointed a Special Envoy for the United Nations Environment Programme (UNEP)
2002	Olympic Order (International Olympic Committee's tribute 'to Sir Peter Blake's outstanding sailing career and to his genuine passion for sport and adventure')

Awards

1982	New Zealand Yachtsman of the Year
1989	New Zealand Sports Personality of the Year
1989–90	Communicator of the Race Award, Whitbread Round-the-World Race
	New Zealand Yachtsman of the Year
	New Zealand Sports Team of the Year (with *Steinlager 2* crew)
1990	ABC 'Wide World of Sports' Athlete of the Week (May)
	Public Relations Institute of New Zealand Communicator of the Year
	Yachting Magazine (USA) Yachtsman of the Year
1994	International Yacht Racing Union World Sailor of the Year (with Robin Knox-Johnston)
	Hobson Medal for excellence in New Zealand Maritime Endeavours

1995	New Zealand Sportsman of the Year (with Team New Zealand)
	New Zealand Outstanding Management and Marketing Achievement Award
	Royal Yacht Squadron Sir Francis Chichester Award (with Robin Knox-Johnston)
	International SeaKeepers' Society SeaKeeper Award 'for extraordinary dedication and leadership in the cause of marine conservation'
2002	Ocean Stewardship Award from the United National Environment Programme
	Laureas World Sports Academy, Lifetime Achievement Award

Yachting achievements

1967–68	Winner, New Zealand Junior Offshore Group championship on *Bandit*
1971	Line honours in inaugural Cape Town to Rio de Janeiro race (watch leader on *Ocean Spirit*)
1973–74	Watch leader on inaugural Whitbread Round-the-World race in *Burton Cutter*
1974	First monohull to complete Two-man Round Britain race with Robin Knox-Johnston on *Burton Cutter*
1977	Line honours in inaugural Two-man Round North Island (New Zealand) with Graeme Eder on *Gerontius*
1977–78	Watch leader on second Whitbread race on *Heath's Condor*
1979	Line honours in Miami to Montego Bay, skipper of *Heath's Condor*
	Line honours and race record in Antigua to Bermuda race, skipper of *Heath's Condor*
	Line honours and race record in Fastnet race, skipper of *Heath's Condor*
1980	Line and handicap double in Sydney to Hobart race, skipper of *Ceramco*
1981–82	Handicap wins in legs 2 and 4 of third Whitbread race, skipper/navigator of *Ceramco*
	Roaring Forties Trophy for best corrected time, legs 2 and 3 on Whitbread race, skipper/navigator of *Condor*
1983	Member, New Zealand Admiral's Cup challenge, skipper/team captain of *Lady B*
1984	Line honours, Sydney to Hobart race, skipper/navigator of *Lion New Zealand*
1985–86	Second fastest, fourth Whitbread race, skipper/navigator of *Lion New Zealand*

1988	Line honours in inaugural Two-man Round Australia race, with Mike Quilter on trimaran *Steinlager 1*
1989–90	Line honours in English Channel Race, skipper of *Steinlager 2*
	Line honours in Fastnet Race, skipper on *Steinlager 2*
	Line and handicap honours, all six legs of Whitbread race, skipper of *Steinlager 2*
	Overall line and handicap honours in Whitbread Race, skipper of *Steinlager 2*
	Roaring Forties Trophy for best corrected time performance in legs 2 and 3 of Whitbread Race
1991–92	Manager of New Zealand America's Cup challenge in San Diego
1993	Contested inaugural Trophée Jules Verne, co-skipper of catamaran *ENZA* (with Robin Knox-Johnston)
1994	Winner, Trophée Jules Verne, setting record circumnavigation of 74 days, 22 hours, 17 minutes, 22 seconds, skipper of catamaran *ENZA*
1992–95	Co-founder (with Alan Sefton) and syndicate head of Team New Zealand
1995	Winner, America's Cup, syndicate head of Team New Zealand Crew on winning boat *NZL32, Black Magic*
1995–2000	Syndicate head, Team New Zealand
2000	Syndicate head of Team New Zealand, winner of America's Cup
	Co-founder (with Alan Sefton and Scott Chapman) and head of blakexpeditions
2001	Inaugural blakexpeditions voyage of exploration to Antarctic
	Second blakexpeditions voyage of exploration 1400 miles up the Amazon and Negro rivers in Brazil

Positions held

President of the Jules Verne Association

Patron of Devonport Yacht Club (New Zealand); Gulf Harbour Yacht Club (New Zealand); Essex Yacht Club (England)

Vice-president of Royal Port Nicholson Yacht Club (New Zealand)

Trustee of New Zealand International Yachting Trust

Life member of Royal New Zealand Yacht Squadron; West Mersea Yacht Club (England)

Honorary member of Royal Yacht Squadron (England); Royal Southampton Yacht Club (England)

Member of Emsworth Sailing Club (England); Ocean Cruising Club (England); Association of Cape Horners

Glossary

battened down   a vessel is battened down for bad weather, i.e. all hatches and doors tightly closed and secure.

Beaufort Scale   a scale describing sea conditions, devised in 1805 by a Royal Navy captain, and widely used in weather forecasting. The scale goes from calm conditions (Force One), through light to strong breeze (Force Eight), to gale, storm, and finally hurricane (Force 12).

Bermudan rig   the most common modern rig for yachts, this is a triangular mainsail sail attached to a mast. It was developed in Bermuda in the 17th century.

broach   a sudden loss of control on a yacht when running or reaching, when the wind's forces become too great and the boat is pushed over towards the horizontal. Without quick, corrective action it can lead to a capsize or 'death roll'.

catamaran   a vessel with two hulls joined by a central platform.

caulking   the sealing used to make wooden decks watertight, traditionally of fibres of cotton or oakum (hemp fibre soaked in tar).

chainplates   a metal plate used to fasten a wire shroud or stay to a yacht's hull.

clinker   a traditional boat-building method, used specially for smaller boats, where the wooden planks overlap.

close-hauled   sailing 'on the wind' or 'close to the wind.'

downwind   sailing with the wind astern.

gunter rig   a rig used on small gaff-rigged sailboats, for example, the P-class dinghy. A gaff rig hoists a sail that has four sides. Gaff rigs were in use before more efficient Bermudan triangular rigs became popular in the 20th century.

going to windward   sailing close-hauled or 'on the wind.'

gybe   a manoeuvre to swing a yacht's boom and sail to the opposite side by bringing the stern through the wind. An uncontrolled or crash gybe can result in a dangerous broach.

hove to   in bad weather a vessel may be hove to, that is, brought up close to the wind and stopped by lowering sails.
in the lee of   in the shelter of, for example, an island or a headland.
ketch   a two-masted yacht with a shorter mast aft.
knock-down   a yacht's position when the wind's forces lay her over to an acute and sometimes dangerous angle.
light displacement   a light displacement yacht is lighter in overall weight and displaces less water than a heavier one.
mizzen   the rear of two masts on a ketch.
monohull   a sailing craft with one hull.
multihull   a sailing craft with two or three hulls.
pitchpoled   when a yacht cartwheels end-over-end.
sloop   a yacht with a single mast, a mainsail and one foresail.
spinnaker   a very large, lightweight and tricky sail used for sailing downwind (wind coming from behind).
spreaders   small horizontal spars attached to a mast to keep the wires (shrouds) holding it upright and securely away from the mast.
step   to 'step' a mast means to erect it on a yacht.